**LONDON, NEW YORK,
MELBOURNE, MUNICH, AND DELHI**

Created by
Chris Ying and Brian McMullen

Assistant Editor Onnesha Roychoudhuri
Assistant Designers Jayme Yen and Lauren LoPrete
Executive Consultant Eli Horowitz

For DK
Project Editor Jenny Finch **Senior Art Editor** Jacqui Swan
Managing Editor Linda Esposito **Managing Art Editor** Diane Thistlethwaite
Publishing Manager Andrew Macintyre **Category Publisher** Laura Buller
DK Picture Library Jenny Baskaya, Rob Nunn **Senior Production Controller** Angela Graef
DTP Designers Maria Elia, Hitesh Patel **Jacket Designer** Yumiko Tahata
Jacket Editor Mariza O'Keeffe

First published in the United States in 2009
by DK Publishing
375 Hudson Street
New York, New York 10014

09 10 11 12 13 10 9 8 7 6 5 4 3 2 1
MD568 – 07/09

There are three penguins in top hats on page 57.

DK books are available at special discounts when purchased in bulk for
sales promotions, premiums, fundraising, or educational use. For details, contact:
DK Publishing Special Markets
375 Hudson Street
New York, New York 10014
SpecialSales@dk.com

A catalog record for this book is
available from the Library of Congress.

ISBN: 978-0-7566-5405-4

Color reproduction by MDP, UK
Printed and bound by Toppan, China

**Discover more at
www.dk.com**

109 FORGOTTEN AMERICAN HEROES

(PLUS NINE OR SO VILLAINS)

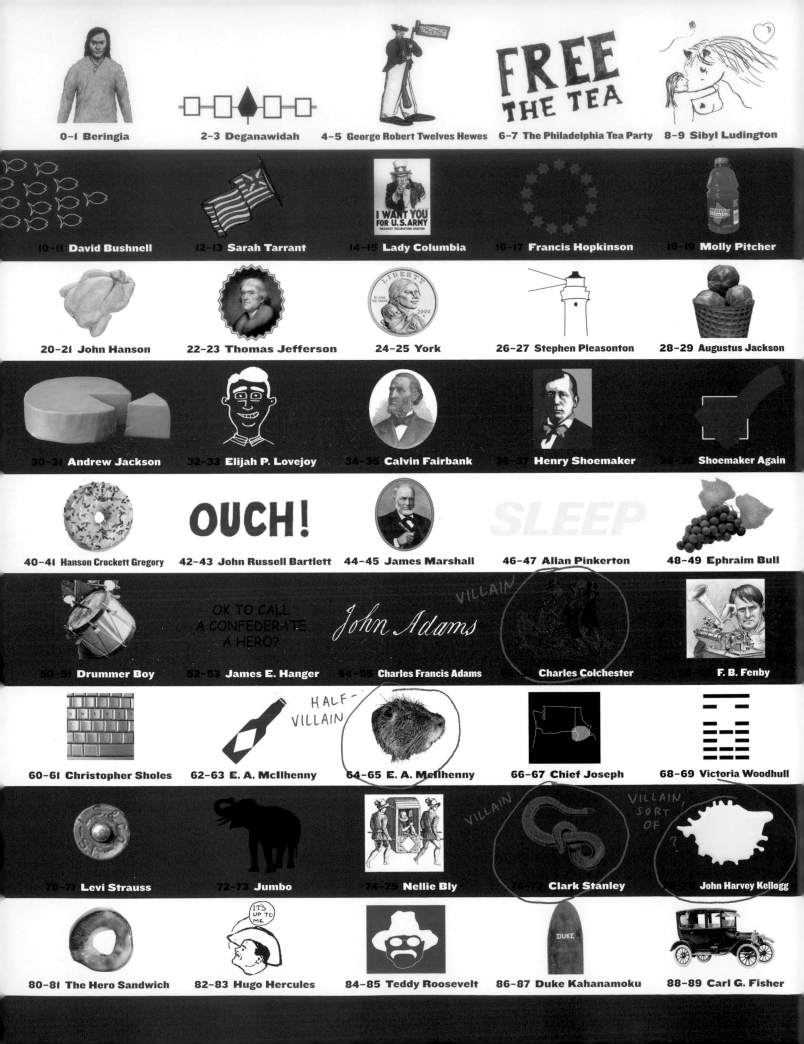

0-1 Beringia

2-3 Deganawidah

4-5 George Robert Twelves Hewes

6-7 The Philadelphia Tea Party

8-9 Sibyl Ludington

10-11 David Bushnell

12-13 Sarah Tarrant

14-15 Lady Columbia

16-17 Francis Hopkinson

18-19 Molly Pitcher

20-21 John Hanson

22-23 Thomas Jefferson

24-25 York

26-27 Stephen Pleasonton

28-29 Augustus Jackson

30-31 Andrew Jackson

32-33 Elijah P. Lovejoy

34-35 Calvin Fairbank

36-37 Henry Shoemaker

38-39 Shoemaker Again

40-41 Hanson Crockett Gregory

42-43 John Russell Bartlett

44-45 James Marshall

46-47 Allan Pinkerton

48-49 Ephraim Bull

50-51 Drummer Boy

52-53 James E. Hanger

54-55 Charles Francis Adams

Charles Colchester

F. B. Fenby

60-61 Christopher Sholes

62-63 E. A. McIlhenny

64-65 E. A. McIlhenny

66-67 Chief Joseph

68-69 Victoria Woodhull

70-71 Levi Strauss

72-73 Jumbo

74-75 Nellie Bly

Clark Stanley

John Harvey Kellogg

80-81 The Hero Sandwich

82-83 Hugo Hercules

84-85 Teddy Roosevelt

86-87 Duke Kahanamoku

88-89 Carl G. Fisher

90-91 Garrett Morgan

92-93 Stephen Mather

94-95 Cher Ami

96-97 Phog Allen

98-99 Beulah Louise Henry

100-101 Frank Epperson

102-103 Richard Drew

104-105 Charles Brannock

106-107 Preservers of Memorials

108-109 Floretta McCutcheon

110-111 Billy Tipton

WORK
112-113 Labor Unions

114-115 Spam

116-117 Josh Gibson

118-119 Navajo Code Talkers

VILLAIN
120-121 Ferdinand Waldo Demara

122-123 John Stapp

124-125 Edwin Land

126-127 Albert I

128-129 Brownie Wise

130-131 Elbert Botts

132-133 Claudette Colvin

HAVE YOU EVER USED ANYTHING?
134-135 Containerization

136-137 Jesse Glover

VILLAIN
138-139 Lester Wunderman

140-141 Harvey Ball

142-143 Shamu

CUBICLE STRESS
144-145 Robert Propst

146-147 Fast Food

148-149 Thompson & Calley

150-151 Michael Collins

152-153 John McConnell

154-155 Ralph Baer

156-157 Patsy Mink

158-159 The Barcode

160-161 Michael Larson

162-163 Mary Rodas

HOME FOR SALE
164-165 Biosphere 2

166-167 Richard Jewell

LIFE WITHOUT ARMS
168-169 Marty Ravellette

170-171 Pluto

172-173 Bertha

174-175 Everyday Heroes

"Of the 4,543,218

have performed acts of heroism in our country's history, 92.4% from the registry at the National Historical Memorial Archive Magnanimity or Selflessness.¹ No one knows where these

1. Situated underground, somewhere along the Appalachian Trail, the Archives are accessible only by guided gharry (see page 75 for more on the gharry). Throughout American history, only fourteen gharry operators have been entrusted with the whereabouts of the Archives: eleven women, two men, and one person named Eng (gender undetermined).

2. OK, that's it for the made-up stuff. The rest of this book—starting now—is all factual. Every hero, every villain, and every joke in these pages is, believe it or not, real.

THE INTRODUCTION TO THIS BOOK

No doubt you have questions. Of course you do. Why would you pick up
a book if you already knew everything there is to know about it?
We're guessing that the questions you have right off the bat are something like these:

What does it mean to be a forgotten American hero?
How does one come to be forgotten?
For that matter, what qualifies a person as a hero?
And you know what—while we're at it—what exactly is an American?

Answers:

A lot.
It just happens, probably.
Doing something heroic.
It's hard to say. *

Thanks for reading the introduction.
Please recycle this book when you are done.

* In this book, we use the word "American" to refer to the United States of America. We don't mean any disrespect to Mexico, Canada, or the countries of Central and South America— all of which are American, and each of which has many forgotten heroes. If we could have used the phrase "United Statesian" without feeling wacky, we would have done it.

Americans who

have been forgotten. Their names and vital data are missing of Persons Performing or Having Performed Feats of Great records have gone, or when they disappeared."

—From an ancient American legend we just made up[2]

Still! You're still here!

Well, if you're just going to *linger* at the beginning, we might as well explain a few things about the folks that populate the rest of this book.

Forgetting a hero isn't the same thing as forgetting to bring your soccer cleats to practice. You knew you were supposed to bring your cleats, but it slipped your mind. You were running out the door and your mom was shouting, "Don't forget your cleats!" but you were thinking about salsa or civil engineering, and you just walked right on out without grabbing them.

Forgetting a hero is something that has almost nothing to do with you. Heroes are forgotten when we never get the chance to learn about them. They're left out of textbooks, and nobody makes movies about them. Or, sometimes they do make movies about them, but we don't see the movies, because they aren't made very well. But then why are some heroes forgotten, when others are not?

Well sometimes we're embarassed. There are heroes like Hugh Thompson, Jr. (148) who stood up for what they believed in, even though what they believed in was unpopular. As a country, we don't really like to be proven wrong, so even if in the end we recognize that we were wrong, we choose to forget the people who

were saying "Hey you're wrong" the whole time.

Other times we forget heroes because other people have done them one better. F.B. Fenby (58) tried to invent the world's first sound-recording device, but couldn't quite get it. Thomas Edison picked up where Fenby left off, succeeded, and is now remembered as the great inventor he was. But that doesn't mean Fenby isn't worth remembering! (Nor should we forget J. E. Hanger (52), a Confederate soldier who was the first amputee of the Civil War. After the good guys took his leg with a cannonball, Hanger devoted the rest of his life to coming up with better and better artificial legs. Thanks, James.)

In this book you'll also see that you can be famous but still forgotten. Take Thomas Jefferson (22), for example. Famous dude. But did you know that ol' T.J. was also the creator of macaroni and cheese? Our third president gave us delightful, delectable mac 'n' cheese!

But the majority of the heroes you'll meet in this book were forgotten simply because we took them for granted. We seldom stop to think about the first people to set foot on North America (0), or the guy who invented tape (102), or carrier pigeons (94), or SPAM (114). Yup, SPAM's a hero, too.

Our forgotten heroes come in all shapes and sizes, and performed feats both large and small. There are heroes whom you might not think of as American— either because they're older than America, or because they're whales (142) or imaginary characters (82)—but we feel that being "American" should mean more than just being born in one of the fifty states. Hopefully after reading this book, you'll know what we mean.

Oh, and the villains. We almost forgot about the villains. The bad guys in this book aren't what you might expect. Most of them are just people who tried hard to do something good, but ended up creating a modern nuisance (144) . But, well, some of them are pretty bad people (120), too....

In any case, we kept the villains to a minimum, because after all, it's the heroes that inspire us. The fact that they're forgotten just adds to their allure. Every time we learn about a new hero, it feels like we're digging up a little piece of hidden treasure. Or a bone. A bone from some long-extinct gigantic duck, with antennae and bulging eyes. Yeah! Imagine American history is this huge, creepy duck, and with each remembered hero, you're unearthing a tiny fragment of its spectacular, mysterious fossil. Eventually you'll rebuild the whole duck, but it's going to take a lot of digging.

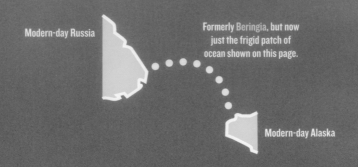

Modern-day Russia

Formerly Beringia, but now just the frigid patch of ocean shown on this page.

Modern-day Alaska

BERINGIA

— AND THE —

PALEOAMERICANS

American heroes before there was an America.

Hey there.

THINK BACK TO YOUR LAST BIRTHDAY PARTY.

Remember it? Was there pizza? Maybe some balloons? That crazy clown... Oh, no clown? Okay, in any case, you remember it.

Now think back a little further. Two birthdays ago. Five birthdays ago. Still remember?

Now try this: Imagine a time before you were born—way before you were born. Before America was a country. Try to imagine a time when the far corner of Asia was connected to Alaska by a small bridge of land, and a group of nomadic people crossed that bridge in search of food. Can you picture it?

When we think about our own lives, it's hard to imagine how things were before we were born. It's the same with American history. We often forget to think about the country before America was born.

But plenty happened before the founding fathers got here. The first humans to arrive came thousands of years before the European explorers and settlers who founded the country. What's more, the path they took is one that will never be possible again. These early travelers are known as Paleoamericans, and the bridge they took is known as Beringia.

During the Ice Age, large parts of the ocean froze, causing the sea level to drop. Beringia emerged from this shallow sea, and connected Asia and North America for nearly 20,000 years, allowing tribes of Paleoamericans to explore all the way from the tip of Alaska to South America.

At the end of the Ice Age, as the snow and ice melted, sea levels rose again and Beringia was covered with water. Today the icy waters of the Bering Strait separate America from Russia. But for a time, man was able to bridge that gap by foot. And, while we may never know what he (or she!) looked like, one Paleoamerican was the very first one to cross over. Along with his or her companions, that person braved the cold and the snow and crossed Beringia into an unknown land where they became the very first people to ever set foot on America, and the first forgotten heroes of American history!

I PLEDGE ALLEGIANCE TO THE FLAG OF THE UNITED TRIBES OF THE IROQUOIS CONFEDERACY...

MOHAWK   ONEIDA   ONONDAGA

WAS THIS THE FIRST REAL FLAG OF THE UNITED STATES?

In some senses, yes. Absolutely. This symbol represents the Iroquois Confederacy, a group of Native American tribes that joined together some time in the 16th century in what is now upstate New York. **DEGANAWIDAH**, a Huron Native American, is the man who first inspired the five original tribes of the Confederacy to band together and make peace. As a young man, Deganawidah had traveled south to seek peace with other tribes. There, he met **HIAWATHA**, a brash, young Huron living with the Mohawks. Deganawidah convinced Hiawatha to join him and use his strong personality for the cause of peace. With Hiawatha as spokesman, the pair convinced the Mohawk to join together with the Oneida, Onondaga, Cayuga, and Seneca tribes. While other tribes had tried similar alliances before, the Iroquois Confederacy (a name actually bestowed upon it by their enenmies; the Iroquois call themselves Hodenosaunee) was the most successful. They were careful in electing leaders and making decisions; they worked together to increase the amount of land they held; and with the threat of colonial invasion looming, they banded together to keep their people safe.

In 1772, the Tuscarora tribe joined the Confederacy, bringing the total number of tribes to six. Soon after, however, U.S. Major General John Sullivan attacked and brought down the Iroquois in 1779. Still, for more than a century before the American Revolution, the Iroquols Confederacy was the strongest union of people on the continent. They kept European countries from fully taking over the country, and were perhaps the first real United States of America.

CAYUGA   **SENECA**   **TUSCARORA**

GEORGE ROBERT TWELVES HEWES IN
"DECISIONS, DECISIONS, DECISIONS"

In the late 1760s, George Robert Twelves Hewes (whew! what a name!) was working as an apprentice shoemaker. When his master's business fell apart, he figured he might as well enlist in the British Army. America was still an English colony at the time, and England was in the middle of fighting the French and Indian War. Why not join the cause? But when George showed up, the British officers scoffed at his height—he was only 5' 1" (1.5m)—and would not let him enlist. Dismayed, George left to try opening his own shoe business.

A few years later, in 1770, tensions were growing between the colonists and the British. One night, Hewes watched a group of British soldiers opening fire on a crowd of protesting colonists. One dying colonist fell into Hewes's arms. George was mortified! He had witnessed what would come to be known as the Boston Massacre.

As the colonists grew more and more dissatisfied with the British, so did Hewes. On December 16, 1773, he joined a group of disguised colonists sneaking aboard a British ship to toss the cargo into the ocean as a protest over tea taxes. Sound familiar? Yep, it was the Boston Tea Party. (Turn the page for more tea party fun.)

After that, little George Hewes continued to play a big role in the rebel cause. Once the actual war began, Hewes spent twenty months fighting for the colonists. He even had a special job. George could whistle one heck of a loud whistle. Whenever needed, Hewes could quiet a crowd and get everyone's attention with one single piercing note. And so it came to be that George Robert Twelves Hewes, a man deemed too short to fight for the British, played a larger-than-life part in some of the defining moments of the American Revolution. Never underestimate the abilities of a short person with a big heart!

ON DECEMBER 16, 1773, a group of angry colonists in Boston protested against the unfair taxation of tea by the British. That night, they snuck aboard a ship belonging to the British East India Company, and dumped 342 chests of tea into the harbor. The event came to be known as the Boston Tea Party. Everybody knows that, though. But not everyone knows that it inspired a similar act a few hundred miles away...

THE PLEASURE OF YOUR
PRESENCE IS REQUESTED AT THE

Philadelphia Tea Party

IN RESPONSE TO THE UNFAIR
TAX ON TEA LEVIED UPON US BY

His Highness, The King of England

ON THE 27TH OF DECEMBER, 1773,
"THE TEA SHALL NOT BE LANDED"

Following the example set by our Boston brethren, but with more modesty and discretion, we shall refuse the delivery of tea from England, by threatening to tar and feather the captain of the tea ship *Polly* should he attempt to make his delivery. Immediately following, we will then offer assistance in returning the cargo home without incident.

☐ WILL ATTEND   ☐ WILL NOT ATTEND

...IN PHILADELPHIA, where a group of like-minded colonists felt like they should throw their own, more civilized tea party. Ten days after the Boston Tea Party, upset Philadelphians politely told the captain of the British tea ship *Polly* that if he made his delivery they would cover him in tar and feathers. Of course, when the captain agreed to turn around, the kindly people of Philly helped him on his way.

THE MIDNIGHT RIDE OF ~~PAUL REVERE~~ SIBYL LUDINGTON
BY HENRY WADSWORTH LONGFELLOW

Listen my children and you shall hear
Of the midnight ride of Paul Revere,
On the eighteenth of April, in Seventy-five;
Hardly a man is now alive
Who remembers that famous day and year.

He said to his friend, "If the British march
By land or sea from the town to-night,
Hang a lantern aloft in the belfry arch
Of the North Church tower as a signal light,--
One if by land, and two if by sea;
And I on the opposite shore will be,
Ready to ride and spread the alarm
Through every Middlesex village and farm,
For the country folk to be up and to arm."

Well that sounds all well and good,
But this famous story is misunderstood.
While Revere rode for some distance,
'Twas I who warned the resistance!
Old Pauly did alert Adams and Hancock,
But was caught by Brits and sent to the cellblock.
Nine days later with the British advancing the fight,
I mounted my horse and rode through the night.
I called my neighbors out of their sleep—
A promise to my father I meant to keep.
While dad stayed home to ready his troops,
I rode on to give others the scoop.
Forty miles, from dusk till dawn,
Through cold and fear, I rode on.

Yet Paul Revere has gone on to great fame
And forgotten in history has been my name.
I hate that guy.

PAUL

WHAT A JERK!

8

Dear Diary,

Here it's been a month since I made my fateful ride, warning local militiamen of the coming of the Redcoats. Every day, I feel as though Paul Revere's legacy is growing. That's all fine and dandy, I suppose, but I can't help but think: What about me?

I know, I know. I should think of the greater good. But I rode on horseback for forty miles! In the dark! Paul Revere rode from Boston to Lexington. That's only about ten miles! Then, he stopped to have a midnight snack with John Adams and John Hancock. Only after William Dawes showed up and was like, "Hey Paul, you think maybe we should keep going and warn some other people?" did Revere move on.

Then, after they picked up some other guy named Dr. Samuel Prescott, the trio made it just outside of Lexington and were picked up by a group of British soldiers. They were eventually released, but by the time Revere got out, others had picked up where he left off.

Me, for example. I rode forty miles! I'm a sixteen-year-old girl! While my father stayed behind to organize his men (he's a colonel), I rode from house to house knocking on doors with the stick I used to urge my horse on. Of course, there were others doing the same thing all throughout the colonies, but only P.R. gets the credit. Life is sooo unfair.

Sibyl

DAVID BUSHNELL

His Tiny Submarine Revolutionized the Revolutionary War—Almost!

In 1775, a crazy-looking military proposal hit George Washington's desk: A guy named David Bushnell from Connecticut wanted to build a tiny, hand-powered ship that could 1. go completely underwater; 2. approach the side of a British ship, undetected; 3. drill a hole in the ship's hull; 4. plant a timed explosive in the hole; 5. safely and quietly retreat; and 6. watch from afar as the British ship suddenly exploded.

Of the six steps outlined in Bushnell's plan, six sounded wildly implausible. Sure, the idea of submarines had been talked about forever, but the drilling and the "time bomb" were unheard of, and Bushnell had drawn up extensive plans for really getting it done. Washington was unsure about all this, but on the advice of Connecticut governor John Trumbull, he gave Bushnell the money. Thus was the *Turtle* submarine built. And it almost worked!

On the night of September 7, 1776, Ezra Lee—the army soldier who volunteered to pilot the *Turtle*—approached the HMS *Eagle*, one of the British ships moored off of Manhattan and blockading New York City. Lee tried to bore the hole, but got seen before he could get the drill to work. The British sent a rowboat after the *Turtle*, and Lee released the mine, which exploded. The British, who were bewildered by whatever just happened, did not catch Lee. But the *Turtle* experiment was, alas, not repeated.

PS: Although the ambitious *Turtle* was a failure, all was not lost: Bushnell's sneaky underwater mines managed to sink some British ships in 1777.

As for military submarines, these weren't successfully deployed in American combat until almost 100 years later, during the Civil War, when both sides had 'em.

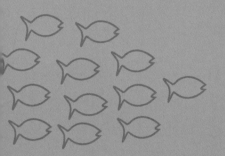

TIME BOMB

It looked much more boring than this— like a small, boring, wooden barrel. No clocks or red dynamite sticks.

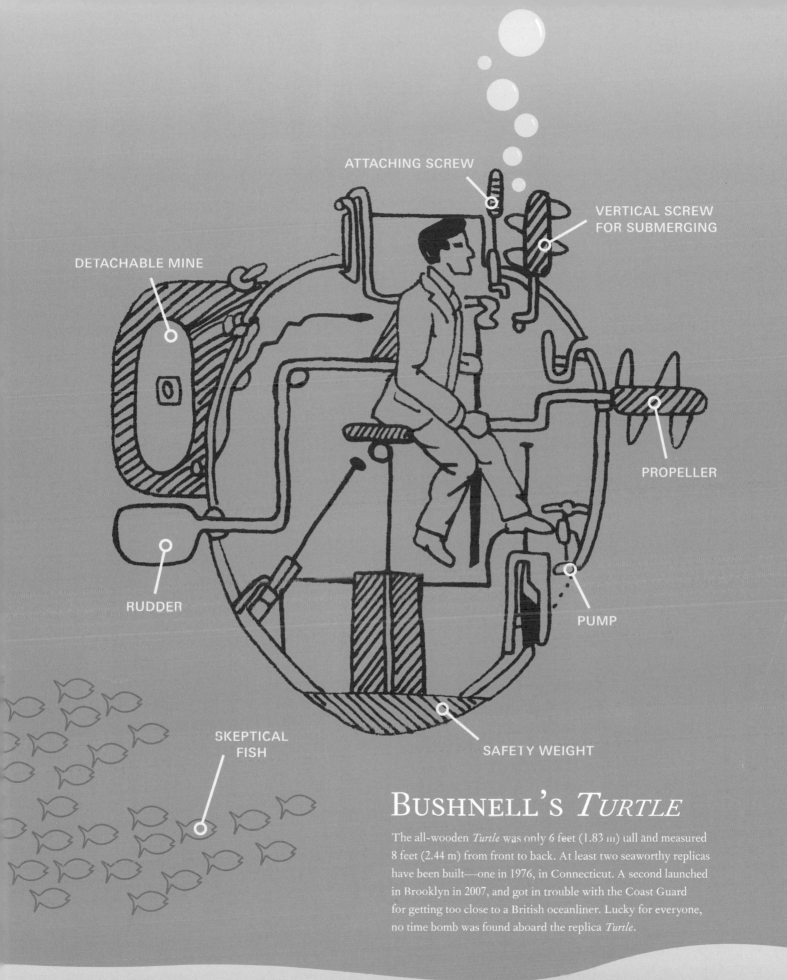

ATTACHING SCREW

VERTICAL SCREW
FOR SUBMERGING

DETACHABLE MINE

PROPELLER

RUDDER

PUMP

SKEPTICAL
FISH

SAFETY WEIGHT

BUSHNELL'S *TURTLE*

The all-wooden *Turtle* was only 6 feet (1.83 m) tall and measured 8 feet (2.44 m) from front to back. At least two seaworthy replicas have been built—one in 1976, in Connecticut. A second launched in Brooklyn in 2007, and got in trouble with the Coast Guard for getting too close to a British oceanliner. Lucky for everyone, no time bomb was found aboard the replica *Turtle*.

SARAH

The Near-Shot That Would

WHAT! DO YOU THINK WE

All of us, at some point or another, learn about the Shot Heard 'Round the World—the first shots fired at the battlefields of Lexington and Concord on April 19, 1775 that set off the American Revolution. But few people know that a nurse in Salem, Massachusetts almost sparked the war a full two months earlier.

In February of 1775, British soldiers (deployed to America to settle the growing discontent among the colonists) passed through Sarah Tarrant's hometown. Their appearance occurred on the Sabbath, the traditional day of rest. The colonists were already on edge, aggravated by the treatment they had received from the British government from across the Atlantic.

As an armed procession of British soldiers in red coats passed by her window, Sarah peered out and yelled to them:

"GO HOME AND TELL YOUR MASTER HE HAS SENT YOU ON A FOOL'S ERRAND, AND BROKEN

THE PEACE OF OUR SABBATH. WHAT! DO YOU THINK WE WERE BORN IN THE WOODS TO BE FRIGHTENED BY OWLS?"

Admittedly, people yell much harsher things all the time today, but this was a pretty big deal back then. A woman was fearlessly standing up to her oppressors!

A soldier raised his musket and took aim at Sarah. Now things were growing tense.

"Fire if you have the courage, but I doubt it," Sarah scoffed.

The soldier backed down. He didn't fire his musket. The battalion went about their way, and the war would have to wait for another day. There were certainly other tense confrontations between colonists and the British, but none resulted in battle until Lexington and Concord.

With a little less luck, Sarah Tarrant might have invited (and possibly been hit by) the Shot Heard 'Round the World.

TARRANT

Have Been Heard 'Round the World

WERE BORN IN THE WOODS TO BE FR

THE COURAGE, BUT I DOUBT IT!

LADY COLUMBIA

"Mother" of Uncle Sam

I WANT YOU FOR U.S. ARMY
NEAREST RECRUITING STATION

MASCOT TO END ALL U.S. MASCOTS?

This super-famous image of Uncle Sam, painted in 1916 by James Montgomery Flagg, was a huge hit when it appeared on Army recruitment posters during World War I. The poster was so beloved that it got used for recruitment again, two decades later, during World War II.

Whenever somebody wants to draw the USA as a human character, they just draw a thin, white-haired man in a loud suit and top hat, and everybody gets it. It's Uncle Sam! He's our country's go-to mascot. The familiar Uncle Sam image has been with us since the 19th century, but he really exploded in popularity during World War I. Uncle Sam became so popular, in fact, that he accidentally forced every other U.S. mascot into retirement!

Perhaps the earliest U.S. mascot of them all (and the most popular, for a while) was "Lady Columbia." Named after Christopher Columbus, Lady Columbia appeared in Revolutionary War poetry in 1776. Later, in 19th century newspapers, she often appeared in editorial cartoons as a beautiful goddess. Although Lady Columbia is pretty much out of commission these days as a patriotic symbol, you shouldn't feel too bad for her. We hear she has her own movie studio now.

This rather striking portrait of Lady Columbia, painted by Paul Stahr in 1917 or 1918, also appeared on patriotic posters during World War I. But for whatever reason, Flagg's painting of Uncle Sam struck that special chord that turned him into America's lone superstar mascot.

INVENTOR, ARTIST, SCHOLAR, MUSICIAN. THERE ARE MANY THINGS THAT WE'RE SURE FRANCIS HOPKINSON WAS. BORN ON SEPTEMBER 21, 1737, HOPKINSON WAS AN ACCOMPLISHED MAN. HE WAS A DEDICATED SERVANT TO THE YOUNG UNITED STATES OF AMERICA. HE WAS A REPRESENTATIVE FROM NEW JERSEY TO THE CONTINENTAL CONGRESS (THE FIRST FORMAL GOVERNMENT OF THE ORIGINAL 13 AMERICAN COLONIES), AND ONE OF THE 56 SIGNERS OF THE DECLARATION OF INDEPENDENCE. BUT WAS HE ALSO THE FIRST POP STAR? AND THE DESIGNER OF OUR NATION'S FLAG?

SO IN A WAY, HOPKINSON'S SONG "MY DAYS HAVE BEEN SO WONDROUS FREE" WAS THE FIRST POP SONG. BUT HE DIDN'T STOP THERE. IN 1780, HE WROTE A LETTER TO CONGRESS ASKING FOR PAYMENT FOR HIS DESIGN OF THE FIRST FLAG OF THE UNITED STATES! OF COURSE, BETSY ROSS USUALLY GETS CREDIT FOR THIS. BUT IT'S ENTIRELY POSSIBLE THAT HOPKINSON HAS BEEN DENIED THE RECOGNITION HE DESERVES AS THE MAN WHO GAVE US THE STARS AND STRIPES!

FRANCIS HOPKINSON

POSSIBLE DESIGNER OF THE 1ST FLAG OF THE UNITED STATES OF AMERICA

BEING ONE OF A HANDFUL OF PEOPLE WHO SIGNED THEIR NAMES TO ONE OF THE MOST IMPORTANT DOCUMENTS IN OUR COUNTRY'S HISTORY MIGHT BE ENOUGH FOR SOME PEOPLE. BUT NOT FOR FRANCIS HOPKINSON. HE WANTED TO BE REMEMBERED FOR SOMETHING ELSE. IN 1788, HE WROTE, "I CANNOT, I BELIEVE, BE REFUSED THE CREDIT OF BEING THE FIRST NATIVE OF THE UNITED STATES WHO HAS PRODUCED A MUSICAL COMPOSITION." WHAT WAS HE TALKING ABOUT? WELL, IN 1759, HOPKINSON WROTE THE FIRST NON-RELIGIOUS SONG IN AMERICAN HISTORY.

CHECK OUT PAGE 2 FOR MORE ON THE FIRST REAL AMERICAN FLAG.

REVOLUTION
CAN MAKE YOU
THIRSTY

MOLLY
PITCHER-ADE
Revolutionary War Blue

32 FL OZ (1 QT) 946 mL

QUENCH YOUR THIRST
LIKE AN AMERICAN HERO

HARNESS THE POWER OF MOLLY.

WITH MOLLY PITCHER-ADE YOU CAN SLAKE YOUR THIRST LIKE THEY DID AT THE BATTLE OF MONMOUNT.

Hard day fighting for independence in your country's revolution? Well, consider this:

On a sweltering June day in 1778, thirsty American revolutionaries turned to Mary Ludwig Hays, whose husband, John, was fighting in the battle as an artilleryman. Mary dutifully carried water back and forth from a nearby well to her husband and other parched soldiers. Mary Hays came to be known as "Molly Pitcher" for her efforts. However, her accomplishments didn't stop at serving thirsty patriots. What's more, legend has it that when Molly's husband was wounded during the battle, she took over his station manning a cannon.

So next time you're in the heat of battle, grab a bottle of Molly Pitcher-Ade, and refuel your passion for independence!

MOLLY PITCHER-ADE
Revolutionary War Blue™

32 FL OZ (1 QT) 946 mL

MY NAME IS JOHN HANSON...

Society has tricked you into believing that George Washington was our country's first president.

But the fact is, I was number one!

Okay, that may not be exactly true. When you wake up, read on and decide for yourself!

John Hanson was the first to declare "a national day of thanksgiving," the precursor to our modern holiday. So, if nothing else, don't we owe him some credit for establishing Turkey Day?

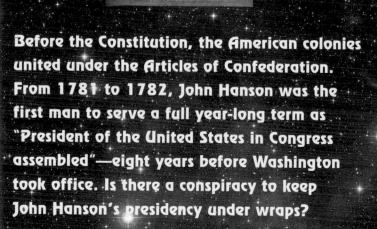

Before the Constitution, the American colonies united under the Articles of Confederation. From 1781 to 1782, John Hanson was the first man to serve a full year-long term as "President of the United States in Congress assembled"—eight years before Washington took office. Is there a conspiracy to keep John Hanson's presidency under wraps?

Under John Hanson's watch, Congress approved the Great Seal of the United States, which is still in use today. Hanson didn't design it, though. That was Charles Thompson. Was Hanson just in the right place at the right time, or is he responsible for one of the most important symbols of our nation?

21

New!!

Macaroni & Cheese

Presidential Flavor

Introducing (to America)

T.J.'s Mac & Cheese

NEW from the third president of the United States comes a wholesome treat for everyone!

As if finalizing the Louisiana Purchase weren't enough, Thomas Jefferson now presents mac & cheese to the U.S.A. Fresh from a recent trip to Italy, T.J. introduces America to its first macaroni machine!

Jefferson Facts

Served as president 1801–1809
Served as president number 3

Birth and Death

Born 1743   Died on July 4, 1826

	%Responsibility*
Declaration of Independence	98%
Signer	1.7%
Author	99%
U.S. Constitution**	1%
Louisiana purchase	100%
Virginia statute for religious freedom	54%
Author	95%
Pushing it into law	2%
Jeffersonian democracy	100%
Founding of University of Virginia	95%
Conception	100%
Architectural planning	100%
Academic/religious separation	100%
Introducing macaroni to the U.S.	100%
Introducing Neo-Palladian architecture	70%

Vitamin A 0%	•	Vitamin B 0%
Calcium 0%		Iron 0%

*Percent responsibility is based on fact as well as arbitrary opinion. You might disagree with how much Thomas Jefferson really had to do with the accomplishments listed above.

**Jefferson was serving as U.S. minister to France during the Constitutional Convention.

SUMMARY: THOMAS JEFFERSON WAS ELECTED THE THIRD PRESIDENT OF THE UNITED STATES, THE SECOND VICE PRESIDENT OF THE UNITED STATES, AND THE FIRST SECRETARY OF STATE. HE IS BEST KNOWN FOR MAKING THE LOUISIANA PURCHASE, WHICH INCLUDED PARTS OF MODERN-DAY ARKANSAS, COLORADO, KANSAS, IOWA, LOUISIANA, MINNESOTA, MISSOURI, MONTANA, NEBRASKA, NEW MEXICO, NORTH DAKOTA, OKLAHOMA, SOUTH DAKOTA, TEXAS, AND WYOMING. HE ALSO FOUNDED THE UNIVERSITY OF VIRGINIA, AUTHORED THE DECLARATION OF INDEPENDENCE, AND FOUGHT FOR THE SEPARATION OF CHURCH AND STATE. BUT MOST IMPORTANTLY, HE BROUGHT THE FIRST MACARONI MACHINE TO THE UNITED STATES OF AMERICA.

T.J.'S MACARONI MACHINE

1 TRAVELS to Italy exposed Jefferson—a renowned lover of fine food and wine—to pasta, specifically macaroni.

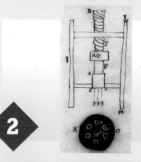

2 DESIGNS for a macaroni machine brought back by Jefferson introduced the dish to diners at the White House.

3 TWO CENTURIES and a few culinary tweaks later, mac & cheese is a staple of American tables.

HI, I'M *YORK*. I WAS A SLAVE ON WILLIAM CLARK'S FAMILY ESTATE IN KENTUCKY, AND THE ONLY BLACK PERSON ASKED TO JOIN LEWIS AND CLARK ON THEIR MISSION TO EXPLORE THE WEST. CLARK AND I WERE ABOUT THE SAME AGE, AND I WAS HIS PERSONAL SERVANT.

WHY WAS I INCLUDED IN THE EXPEDITION? I HAD *SKILLS*! FOR EXAMPLE, UNLIKE MOST OF THE OTHER EXPLORERS, I COULD SWIM. EVEN MY DARK SKIN PROVED TO BE USEFUL. SOME OF THE NATIVE AMERICANS WE ENCOUNTERED HAD NEVER SEEN A BLACK MAN BEFORE, AND OFFERED US HELP BECAUSE THEY THOUGHT I WAS A *GOD*!

I'M *SACAGAWEA* AND I WAS THE ONLY WOMAN IN THE PERMANENT CREW OF THE CORPS OF DISCOVERY. MY BABY, JEAN-BAPTISTE, WAS THE GROUP'S YOUNGEST TRAVELER. USING MY LANGUAGE SKILLS AND KNOWLEDGE OF THE LAND, I HELPED LEWIS AND CLARK CHART THE *GREAT UNKNOWN WEST*!

HEY DON'T FORGET ABOUT ME!

WASSUP! I'M MERIWEATHER LEWIS. IN LATE MAY OF 1804, AT THE REQUEST OF PRESIDENT THOMAS JEFFERSON, WILLIAM CLARK AND I LED A GROUP OF 40 MEN, KNOWN AS THE **CORPS OF DISCOVERY,** ON AN EXTRAORDINARY MISSION TO MAP THE VAST, STILL-UNEXPLORED TERRITORIES OF THE WESTERN UNITED STATES.

DURING OUR VOYAGE, WE GAVE YORK A GREAT DEAL OF RESPONSIBILITY AND FREEDOM. HE HAD *A GUN AND A VOTE.* BUT WHEN WE RETURNED, I DIDN'T RELEASE HIM FROM SLAVERY FOR YEARS. LITTLE IS KNOWN OF THIS FORGOTTEN HERO'S LIFE AFTER HIS RELEASE, EXCEPT THAT HE DIED SOMETIME AROUND 1832, FORGOTTEN BY ALL BUT THE MEN OF THE CORPS OF DISCOVERY.

HEY EVERYONE, WILLIAM CLARK HERE.

In CONGRESS July 4-ish, 1776

The ultimate Declaration of the thirteen united States of America

When in the course of, you know, everyday things happening (birthday parties and grocery shopping, et cetera) it becomes necessary for one, uh, group of guys and gals to break away from those British dudes on the other side of the world, who were totally okay for a while, but then sort of became more and more of a bummer, that group of oppressed people should totally consider declaring themselves independent and be their own country, you know what I mean?

So we hold these truthitudes to be most obvious, that everybody is created the same, and that they all deserve some inalienable rights, like, oh, say, the right to Life? Liberty? The right to wear their hair in pigtails? Shoot, what else? Anyway, the King of Great Britain is definitely not giving us much in the way of alien rights. Here's a list of some of the bogus things he's pulling on us:

He always says he's going to let us pass our own laws, but then at the last second he changes his mind and forgets about us.

He has refused to water the plants when we are away for the weekend, even though he totally promised he would.

Taxes! What is the deal with all of these taxes? Am I right? What else…

The Declaration of Independence, Theoretical Edition
Written from memory by some guy after the original was destroyed.

c. 1814
Ink on Parchment

Two years into the War of 1812, the British were mounting an attack on the American capital. James Monroe, the Secretary of State at the time, received word of the British advance and traveled to the small seaside village where the British were landing, so he could see what we were up against. Upon arriving, he was convinced that we didn't stand a chance. He sent warning back to Washington, where it fell upon a lower-level clerk named Stephen Pleasonton to see to the safety of important State Department documents. Pleasonton sought the advice of the Secretary of War, who told him not to worry so much. "Chill out," he probably said.

Pleasonton was not comforted. He packed up various documents, including the journals of Congress, letters from George Washington, correspondence from officers of the Revolutionary War, and various other treaties, laws, and letters. He had the whole package shipped to a mill in Virginia. As he was surveying the now empty office he was sitting in, he noticed that hanging right in front of his face was none other than the Declaration of Independence. Good grief! He packed it up and took it with him to the mill in Virginia. When he arrived, Pleasonton decided that the mill was not secure enough. He gathered all of the documents he had rescued, including the Declaration, and brought them to an empty house outside of Leesburg. He went to sleep happy with what he had accomplished.

The next morning, Pleasonton awoke to news that Washington had indeed been burned to the ground. Had Pleasonton not saved the Declaration of Independence, American schoolchildren might very well be visiting a silly remake like the one on the opposite page. Thanks, Steve!

BY THE WAY...

Stephen Pleasonton is probably better known for his work as one of the early superintendents of lighthouses in the United States, a post he held for more than thirty years.

AUGUSTUS JACKSON
THE ICE CREAM MAN

THE FATHER OF ICE CREAM?

Augustus Jackson didn't invent ice cream. Let's get that out of the way. He didn't invent the ice cream cone, either. That honor goes to Agnes Marshall, another forgotten hero of frozen confections. So what makes Jackson so special?

In the early 1800s, Augustus was working as a chef at the White House. Around 1830, he decided to set out on his own as a candy manufacturer in Philadelphia. That's when he started messing with ice cream. He invented several ice cream recipes and a method of manufacturing the sweet delight that made it easier and more affordable to produce. He brought ice cream to the masses! And as a result, now he's known as the father of ice cream.

Check out the next page for thoughts on where we'd be if Jackson had never perfected ice cream. It's scary to think about, isn't it?

WHAT IF...

THE NAKED CONE

As much a hat as a food.

THE BASEBALL CONE

It's round, if a little chewy.

SARDINE BALL

Not quite as refreshing as ice cream, but full of protein, which is always a plus, right?

FROZEN MEATBALL

Doesn't go well with hot fudge, admittedly.

ICE CUBE CONE

Cold and... well, that's it. Cold.

THE SPROUT

Most likely.

Andrew Jackson's
BIG WHEEL OF CHEESE

IN 1835, THE DAIRYMEN OF OSWEGO COUNTY, New York sent a 1,400-lb (635-kg) wheel of cheddar—about 4 feet (1.2 m) high and 2 feet (.6 m) thick—as a gift to President Andrew Jackson. Twenty-four gray horses brought the cheese on a cart to the capital. The cheese stood alone in the White House lobby for two years, aging, until February 1837, when Jackson held his last big party in office. He opened the White House doors to the public, and local stores and offices closed up early so that people could attend. People were so eager that they clambered over walls, and snuck through gardens to get a taste. Soon, all that was left of the cheese was the pungent aroma of cheddar, and sizable stains on the carpet.

WHAT'S THIS GOT TO DO WITH AMERICAN HISTORY? Presidents are remembered for a great number of things, but seldom something so simple and so memorable as having a gigantic block of cheese. Jackson was a populist, meaning he believed in connecting with the average man. And what better way is there to connect than over a gigantic hunk of the finest New York cheddar?

BENJAMIN PERLEY POORE, a journalist at the scene, created this depiction of the cheese feast in the White House lobby.

NO CHEESE GRATERS NEEDED: The giant wheel of cheddar was cut with saw blades and, in only two hours, had been demolished by hungry citizens.

Elijah P. Lovejoy

He laid down his life to defend his belief in free speech.

"We distinctly avow it to be our settled purpose, never, while life lasts, to yield to this new system of attempting to destroy, by means of mob violence, the right of conscience, the freedom of opinion, and of the press."

On November 7, 1837, a pro-slavery mob attacked the warehouse in Alton, Illinois where Elijah P. Lovejoy was secretly keeping his new printing press—a replacement for the others that had been destroyed. The attack resulted in Lovejoy's murder.

Some have called Lovejoy "America's first martyr to the freedom of the press."

A devout Presbyterian, Lovejoy wrote angry screeds against the Pope and Catholicism, but no hero is perfect—even in the United States of America. Focus on the good stuff about people, please.

Twenty-four years before the Civil War broke out, an early battle in the war against slavery was fought on the east bank of the Mississippi River. On the night of November 7, 1837, Elijah P. Lovejoy—an abolitionist minister and newspaperman from Alton, Illinois—was killed by an angry mob because he refused to stop publishing his anti-slavery views.

In the two years before he died, Lovejoy's printing press was destroyed a whopping five times (and thrown into the river at least three of those times, for effect). Every time his press was destroyed, Lovejoy replaced it. The nerve!

"THE FIVE PRINTING PRESSES *of* ELIJAH P. LOVEJOY"

AS TOLD *by* THREE ANGRY MOB LEADERS *and a* RACIST JUDGE

In 1834, this Lovejoy yahoo began publishing the *St. Louis Observer*—a weekly "newspaper," if you want to call it that. (Personally, I liked to wipe my dog's butt with it.) Anyway, Lovejoy liked to yak in there about slavery being bad for Missouri. Pshaw! The final straw came in 1836, when he wrote a big sob story about the mob lynching of Frank McIntosh, a free black man. He blabbed about how terrible it was that the honorable Judge Luke E. Lawless let us mob leaders go home, scot free. The story got a lot of us true Americans real hot, so we got together and smashed up Lovejoy's first printing press. And boy—Lovejoy flew out of town in a hurry!

So then Lovejoy comes east to the "free" state of Illinois, where they act so goody-goody—too good for slaves! Lovejoy thought he could publish a new newspaper—the *Alton Observer*—in Alton, Illinois without anybody crudding it up. Gah, ha! Wrong! As soon as Lovejoy's new press arrived on the dock, my buddies and me bashed it to bits and chucked the bitty little pieces into the water. What a riot! You shoulda seen the coward's face. Haw haw haw haw haw! Oh, me....

Between you and me, I think Lovejoy was a little soft in the old melon. After a bunch of local nincompoops raised money for a third press, we let Lovejoy publish his little paper for awhile—fine. But then about a year went by, and he forgot all the lessons we'd taught him. On July 6, 1837, Lovejoy published his strongest-ever condemnation of slavery. That night, we took care of press number three.

Mr. Lovejoy's fourth press was destroyed by a so-called "mob" as soon as it (the press) arrived. I thought that would settle things. But instead of finally taking a hint, Lovejoy went the other way. He organized a militia to secretly buy and install a fifth printing press. But the secret got out. On the night of November 7, 1837, Lovejoy's warehouse was mobbed by some of the gentlemen who have just illuminated this story for you. The militia fought the mob, killing a man. A fire was set, and Lovejoy died trying to extinguish the blaze. If you ask me, Lovejoy's killers probably acted in self-defense. Lovejoy was buried on November 9, his 35th birthday. Tsk, tsk. What a shame.

HON. JUDGE LUKE E. LAWLESS

Calvin Fairbank
Abolitionist Minister

One of the many forgotten heroes of the Underground Railroad, Calvin Fairbank was born in 1816, and developed an early disgust with the practice of slavery. As a child, he listened to slaves tell their stories of hardship, and was convinced of the inherent evils of enslaving other people.

In 1837, he took action. While on a raft on the Ohio River, he spotted a black slave on the Virginia side of the river. He told the man to climb aboard, and ferried him to the free land of the Ohio side of the river. This became Fairbank's life's work. In total, he helped free more than forty-five men and women from bondage. He would retrieve them from southern states, disguise them, and smuggle them to Ohio, where other people would be waiting to bring them to safer destinations in the North, or in Canada.

Like others who worked as part of the Underground Railroad, Fairbank had to keep his activities hidden. As a minister, he would occasionally preach or lecture on his anti-slavery views, but by and large his work was secret.

However, shortly after being ordained a Methodist elder, Fairbank was arrested and tried for freeing slaves. He was sentenced to fifteen years in prison, of which he served four before being pardoned. In 1851, two years after he got out of prison, he was kidnapped and sent to Kentucky, where he was tried again and sentenced to an additional fifteen years in prison.

This time he was in prison until 1864 before being pardoned. After he got out, Fairbank remained a critic of slavery. Before his death, he published an autobiography titled *Rev. Calvin Fairbank During Slavery Times: How He "Fought the Good Fight" to Prepare "The Way,"* which detailed his efforts to free Southern slaves.

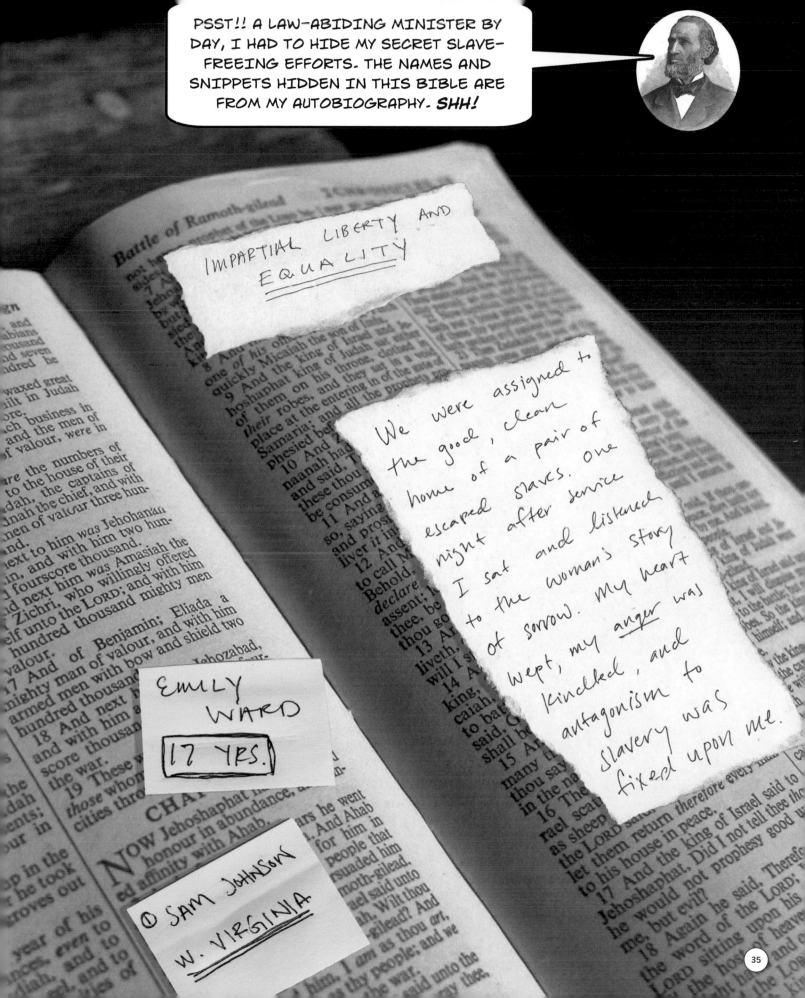

WHY VOTE?

CONSIDER, FOR A MOMENT, THESE MEN:

HENRY SHOEMAKER
MADISON MARSH &
EDWARD HANNEGAN

WHAT

IN THE WORLD ARE WE TALKING ABOUT?

HENRY SHOEMAKER WAS A FARM WORKER LIVING IN INDIANA. ON ELECTION DAY IN 1842, HENRY ALMOST FORGOT TO VOTE. BUT HE'D PROMISED A MAN NAMED MADISON MARSH THAT HE WOULD VOTE FOR HIM FOR STATE REPRESENTATIVE. SO INSTEAD OF TAKING THE LAZY ROUTE, HENRY CAST HIS VOTE. AND AS IT TURNS OUT MARSH WON BY ONE SINGLE VOTE. AND BACK THEN, STATE REPRESENTATIVES CHOSE U.S. SENATORS, SO IN JANUARY OF 1843, MARSH VOTED FOR EDWARD HANNEGAN (THE GUY ON THE PREVIOUS PAGE). HANNEGAN WON BY, YOU GUESSED IT, ONE SINGLE VOTE. FAST FORWARD TO 1846, THE U.S. SENATE IS DEBATING WHETHER WE'D GO TO WAR WITH MEXICO. THE SENATORS VOTE AND HANNEGAN'S VOTE IS THE DECIDING ONE: WAR. IF IT WASN'T FOR OUR VICTORY, WE PROBABLY WOULDN'T HAVE A CALIFORNIA, NEVADA, OR UTAH (NOT TO MENTION PARTS OF ARIZONA, NEW MEXICO, COLORADO, AND WYOMING). IT MIGHT BE A BIT GENEROUS TO SAY THAT HENRY SHOEMAKER IS THE REASON WHY WE HAVE CALIFORNIA, BUT HE DEFINITELY DID MAKE A DIFFERENCE. THAT'S WHY, WHEN YOU TURN EIGHTEEN, YOU MUST

REMEMBER THE IMPORTANCE OF ONE SINGLE...

VOTE

WHO PUT THE HOLE IN THE DOUGHNUT?
HANSON CROCKETT GREGORY.

*"We have built our civilization with Archimides' lever,
Newton's law of gravitation, Franklin's electricity;
yet what would it be without Gregory's doughnut?"*

—THE LITERARY DIGEST, 1916

WHO WAS HANSON CROCKETT GREGORY?
He was a ship captain from Rockport, Maine.

WHEN DID HE PUT THE HOLE IN THE DOUGHNUT?
Sometime around 1847.

HOW DID HE DO IT, AND WHY?
There are three stories, at least.

WHAT'S THE FIRST STORY?
Brrrr! It's a stormy day at sea, and Gregory is eating an *olykoek*—a Dutch-style fried cake. But then oops, he slips, loses his footing, and accidentally slams the cake onto a spoke of the ship's wheel. Eureka! From this point forward, Gregory orders the ship's cook to prepare all fried cakes with holes in the middles, so that he can keep them handy on the helm.

WHAT'S THE SECOND STORY?
Gregory likes to eat fried cakes. Plus, he's a fun-loving guy. So he asks the ship's cook to make novelty cakes in the shape of tiny life preservers. The end.

OPTIONAL DRAMATIC TWIST ADDED BY SOME STORYTELLERS:

Gregory is inspired to ask his cook for life preserver-shaped cakes after losing six men overboard in a terrible storm. According to this version of the tale, the men sank because they'd eaten too many fried cakes! So the holey cakes were devised as a kind of tasty (and lighter-weight) safety reminder.

WHAT'S THE THIRD STORY?
Gregory loves his mom's fried cakes, but she can never get the centers to cook without burning the outsides. Thus, Gregory develops the habit of poking out the uncooked centers of his mom's cakes. Eventually, Gregory's mom starts making cakes with holes in the middles, and the good idea spreads.

WHICH STORY IS TRUE?
That's a good question. If you figure it out, we'll fly you and a friend to any doughnut in the USA.

JOHN RUSSELL BARTLETT ★

heroic wrangler of America's words

worked for more than 30 years to perfect his *Dictionary of Americanisms* (1848), a pioneering book that aimed to describe as many American-born words and phrases as possible. The 412-page first edition was a hit. By the time the 813-page fourth and final edition was published 29 years later, Bartlett's work had opened thousands of eyes to the rich and sprawling beauty—or *ugliness*, some said—of American English.

Please enjoy these 24 words and phrases from the *Dictionary of Americanisms*—there's something here for just about every letter of the alphabet. (Americans hadn't developed many juicy "X" or "Z" words back then. Sorry.)

★ Not to be confused with John "no middle name" Bartlett, who edited *Familiar Quotations* (1855), a hefty collection of quotes by famous people that remains a bestseller today. INTERESTING FACT: Both John Bartletts were 19th-century American publishers of groundbreaking books, and both had the fanatical habit of collecting and ordering words, but neither John Bartlett had anything to do with the 18th-century cultivation of the Bartlett pear.

SPEAKING OF QUOTATIONS: "The new circumstances under which we are placed call for new words, new phrases, and for the transfer of old words to new objects. An American dialect will therefore be formed." —THOMAS JEFFERSON, 1813

absquatulate
"To run away; to abscond."

barbecue
"A term used in the Southern States... for dressing a hog whole, which, being split to the backbone, is laid flat upon a large gridiron, and roasted over a charcoal fire."

chunky
"Short and thick; often applied to the stature of a person."

donation
"That which is given or bestowed; a gift, a grant."

eyes peeled
"On the alert."

flunk
"To fail utterly in a college examination."

go it alone
"Often used of any venture where no aid is asked or needed." (comes from the card game Euchre)

hoodlum
"A ragamuffin; a rough fellow. A California word."

immigrant

"A person who removes into a country for the purpose of a permanent residence."

QUILTING BEE

"Or Quilting frolic. An assemblage of women who unite their labor to make a bed-quilt. They meet by invitation, and in a few hours complete it. Tea follows, and the evening is sometimes closed with dancing or other amusements."

jamboree

"A frolic; a row; a jollification."

rambunctious

"Quarrelsome."

keep a stiff upper lip

"To continue firm, keep up one's courage."

SOCDOLAGER

"A conclusive argument; and figuratively, in a contest, a heavy blow, which shall bring it to a close."

looney

"A foolish fellow."

tend

Comes from the phrase "To attend."

maverick

"Many years ago, a large cattle-owner named Maverick neglected to brand his yearlings, whence they were called 'Mavericks'. Other persons... put their own brands upon them, and thus became their owners. The term Maverick for unbranded yearlings is still preserved throughout [Texas]."

up a tree

"To be cornered; to fail in an undertaking."

never say die

"Do not despair under any circumstances."

valedictorian

"The student of a college who pronounces the valedictory [farewell] oration at the annual commencement."

OUCH!

"An exclamation of pain. Much used in the South."

wamble-cropped

"Sick at the stomach; and, figuratively, crestfallen, humiliated."

PLAY POSSUM

"To deceive.... The opossum, when attacked, pretends to be dead, and thus often deceives his pursuers."

you bet

"The most positive manner of affirmation. Be assured, certainly."

JAMES MARSHALL

"BOYS, I BELIEVE I HAVE FOUND A GOLD MINE!"

The year is 1848. James Wilson Marshall of New Jersey is thirty-eight years old. He's a carpenter by trade, a skill he learned from his old man. When he was eighteen, he left home for Fort Leavenworth, Kansas to try his hand at farming for a little bit. Famine forced him to move to Indiana, then Illinois, but he still didn't have much luck. So, in 1844, Marshall hitched a ride on a wagon headed to California. He ended up at the Sacramento River settlement, where he found work as a carpenter. Things were looking up for a while—Marshall got himself a few hundred acres of land and some livestock. But the luck didn't last long. His cattle were stolen and he was forced to sell his ranch. As fate would have it though, a man named John Sutter was building a sawmill on the American River in Coloma, California, and needed a partner. Marshall agreed to operate the mill for Sutter, in exchange for a share of the lumber. And so the two of them set to work turning trees to wood, unaware that they had set in motion a series of events that would change America forever.

James Marshall and John Sutter never grew rich from the discovery of gold at their sawmill on the American River. In fact, most people who flooded to the West in search of their fortunes were disappointed. Mining for gold had its costs, and if men didn't hit the jackpot, they'd have nothing to show but some used gear and dirty clothes. Moreover, the young West wasn't ready for the flood of settlers and miners. Small towns exploded into full cities. By 1850, San Francisco's population had grown from about 1,000 to 35,000. As a result, disease and crime spread rapidly throughout the region.

SUTTER'S MILL

"GOLD! GOLD! GOLD FROM THE AMERICAN RIVER!"

On January 24, 1848, luck finally shined on Marshall again. While working on the banks of the south fork of the American River, Marshall spotted something shiny in the water. At first, he thought it was just a bit of quartz, but further downstream, he saw bigger yellowish nuggets. He picked one up and pounded it between two rocks. It flattened into a lustrous sheet. "Boys, I believe I have found a gold mine!" he told his fellow workers. The men began mining for gold in their spare time. Sutter and Marshall tried to keep the whole thing under wraps, but gold fever was impossible to suppress. A big mouth named Sam Brannan who worked nearby carried a vial of gold flakes back to San Francisco and yelled, "Gold! Gold! Gold from the American River!" to anyone who would listen. The California Gold Rush had begun. Thousands flocked to Coloma. But as Marshall couldn't get legal recognition of his own gold claim, he was never able to make much off of his discovery. All the workers left the sawmill to look for gold, and the business fell apart. He spent the rest of his life wandering around California impoverished by his discovery.

1848

The discovery of gold at Sutter's Mill created the American West. Legendary figures were born from James Marshall's lucky break: Buffalo Bill, Kit Carson, Calamity Jane, Annie Oakley. Levi Strauss even created the modern blue jean in response to the Gold Rush (check out page 70). But of course, the importance of Marshall's discovery does not stop at the Gold Rush. After the gold-seekers had given up and moved on, many decided not to leave. These people, diverse in background, stayed on and settled the West. So were it not for James Marshall, would California still just be full of bears and unmined gold?

THE COOPER WHO CAUGHT COUNTERFEITERS

In 1842, Scotsman and professional barrel-maker Allan Pinkerton emigrated to Dundee, Illinois, a suburb of Chicago. One day in 1846, while felling trees on a nearby deserted island, Pinkerton spied a charred patch of earth. Suspicious, he teamed up with the local sheriff, and the two men caught a band of counterfeiters who'd been using the island as a hideout! The island has been called "Bogus Island" ever since.

AMERICA'S FIRST PRIVATE DETECTIVE

Pinkerton, the son of a police officer, was so good at detecting that he was appointed deputy sheriff, and soon he became the first detective on the Chicago police force. Then, in 1850, he started the Pinkerton National Detective Agency—the first private detective agency anywhere—and became famous for catching train robbers and hunting outlaws like the Reno Brothers and Jesse James.

Some of Pinkerton's signature work methods, such as "shadowing" suspects and conducting work undercover, were widely copied. To this day, Pinkerton's innovative tactics remain central to detective work.

PINKERTON HAD A GOOD LOGO. The expression "private eye" comes from Pinkerton's company logo: an open eye accompanied by the words "We Never Sleep." Chicagoans in the know called Pinkerton "the Eye."

DID YOU SAY *SECRET* SERVICE?

In 1861, Pinkerton discovered a Confederate plot to assassinate Abraham Lincoln, who had just been elected president. Thinking quickly, Pinkerton organized an alternate railroad route for Lincoln to travel, foiling the plot. It was all in a day's work. The great detective went on to organize a Secret Service Department for Union General George McClellan—a protective entourage that served as the model for the United States Secret Service. The Secret Service was officially founded after Lincoln's assassination in 1865.

ONE DEDICATED DETECTIVE

In the early days of the Civil War, Pinkerton and his agents traveled throughout the South to report on Confederate plans and seek out Union sympathizers. Pinkerton was one dedicated detective. On a rainy summer day in 1861, he took off his boots and stood on the shoulders of his coworkers to get a peek inside the home of Rose O'Neal Greenhow, a wealthy Confederate spy. Teetering on the shoulders, Pinkerton watched, furious and silent, as a traitorous Union soldier—Captain Ellison—delivered a Union Army map and other secrets to Greenhow. When Ellison came out of the house, Pinkerton chased after him in his socks. Ellison's goose was cooked.

SLEEP"

ALLAN PINKERTON'S
SCARY MOTTO

In the photo below, Allan Pinkerton keeps a sleepless, bloodshot eye on President Lincoln in Antietam, Maryland on October 3, 1862.
(Pinkerton is on the left, but I bet you already figured that out.)

HIS DEEDS CAN'T ALL BE GREAT. In the late 1800s, Pinkerton's Agency developed a bad reputation after violently breaking up strikes and fighting unions who sought better wages and safer working conditions.

EPHRAIM BULL

He spent years cultivating the first great American grape — the Concord grape — and then watched, helpless, as competitors grafted the vines and grew grapes by the millions. *Ephraim Bull grew the grape, but other men grew rich!*

(Did this reversal of fortune bother Bull? Yes — it haunted him all the way to the grave. Check out the last line of his epitaph, below.)

Mr. E. Bull of Concord, Mass spent six years breeding us from a strain of wild "northern fox" grapes he found in his back yard in 1843.

Before we Concords came along and changed everything, there was very little grape agriculture in the U.S.

It was just too hard to get European grapes to thrive stateside, and European grapes were regarded as the only grapes worth eating.

We're Concord grapes.

Unlike Bull, most horticulturalists would turn their noses up at native grapes like the fox.

If you're wondering where the U.S. Patent Office was during the wholesale theft of my sweet globular dream, ask that "hero" Thomas Jefferson. When he wrote the country's patent laws, he excluded life forms! Thanks a rotten bunch, T.J. Swell-o.

I grew more than 22,000 seedlings in my lifelong quest for great grapes. Just 21 of those seedlings were worth a darn. (I was a terrible stickler!) The Concord was among the acceptable 0.1%.

What made the Concord so great? Simple. Hardiness and flavor. The Concord was the first grape tough enough to survive outdoors in New England's harsh climate and also tasty enough so Americans actually wanted to eat it. Bingo.

When my Concord grape debuted in 1853, it floored all the grape nerds. They thought it was a hoax, my grapes were so big and juicy. I made big bucks that year — $3,200 — selling my vines to hobbyists. But sales crashed. Farmers started growing huge quantities, and the U.S. grape industry was born. And me? I was left in the dust!

I'm Bull.
"Gold pounding" (making gold leaf) was my trade, but grapes were my lifelong passion.

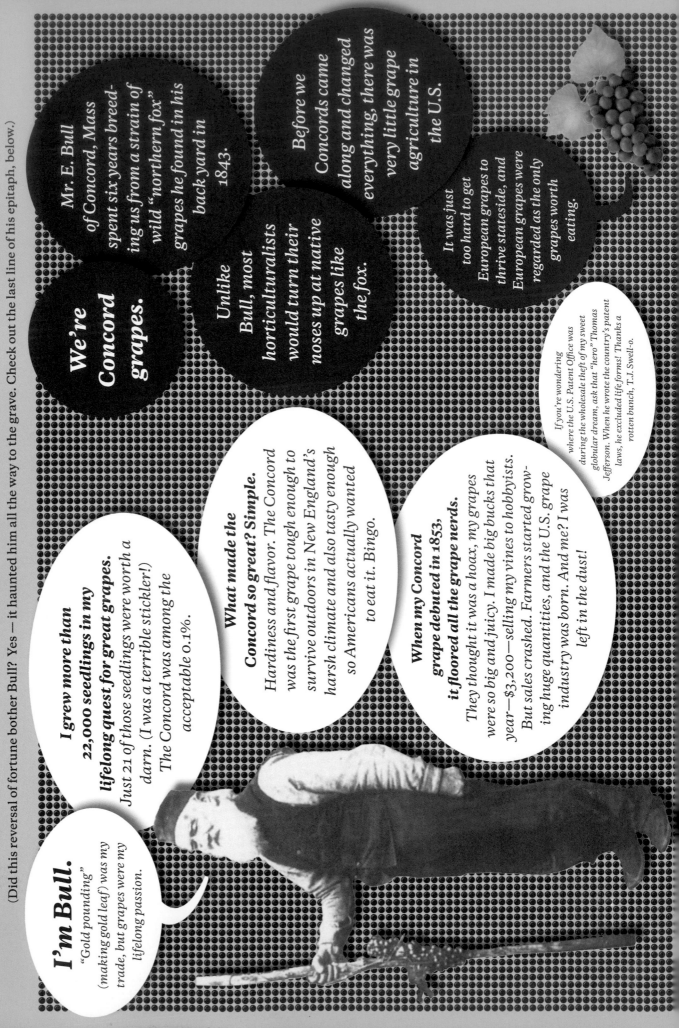

DRUMMER BOY

Robert Henry Hendershot was barely a teenager when he joined the Union Army during the Civil War. Like many other boys of his age, he served as an infantry drummer boy. In both the American Revolution and the Civil War, boys as young as ten would enlist and serve as drummers. Their duty was to lay down the beat to which the regiment would march forth into battle. Different beats would alert fellow soldiers when it was time to change formations or retreat from the battlefield.

50

But the work of these young soldiers didn't stop at laying down beats during battle. They passed down the day-to-day orders for the infantry and, in the heat of battle, Robert Hendershot and his fellow drummer boys would often pick up arms. During one fight, Robert's drum was smashed to pieces. Dutifully, he picked up a rifle and set to fighting for the North. Our hero even managed to capture a Confederate soldier. It's all part of the job when you're a drummer boy doing the work of a drummer man!

JAMES EDWARD HANGER

INNOVATOR *in* ARTIFICIAL LEG DESIGN

*The Hanger Leg
(1891 version)*

The hinged, shock-absorbing knee incorporated an internal bracket that helped the leg bend back and forth more naturally than some other prosthetic legs.

The padded socket piece conformed to the shape of the leg stump. The padding would self-adjust with the movements of the wearer.

On June 1, 1861, James Edward Hanger was a college student who'd just shelved his books to fight for the Confederacy in the Civil War. Two days later, he found himself at the wrong end of a cannon in the war's first land battle—the Battle of Philippi, West Virginia—and he lost his left leg. Hanger became the first amputee of the Civil War.*

Not one to mope, Hanger returned home to Virginia and searched for a good artificial leg. Dissatisfied with the options, he fashioned one from scratch out of wooden barrel pieces, using a spare hinge for the knee. The leg was the first in a decades-long series of "Hanger Legs."

The foot was a separate piece that interlocked with the leg. The foot was cushioned by "elastic bumpers."

In 1864, the Confederacy, suitably impressed by Hanger's craftsmanship and also his dramatic cannonball-to-the-leg story, contracted Hanger to build prosthetic legs for fellow amputee veterans. A contract with the state of Virginia followed in 1867. The legs received mixed reviews at first—some of them had been produced quickly and sloppily, and got tossed aside by vets who preferred their trusty peg-legs—but Hanger's lucrative contract with the state allowed him to keep improving the design.

Hanger's leg received a patent in 1891, and business thrived. By 1918, Hanger's popular artificial legs (and arms) were available through a chain of Hanger storefronts throughout the United States, as well as in Paris and London. Hanger grew rich, but he never forgot where the wealth came from. In the parlor of his home, he kept a curious decoration on prominent display: a six-pound cannonball.†

---

* After Hanger, roughly 60,000 more soldiers would receive amputations during the Civil War—30,000 on each side. The demand for artificial limbs among veterans led to a golden period of innovation in prosthetics.

† 6 pounds = 2.7 kilograms. But Hanger didn't care about kilograms.

Hi, Reader—

John Adams here, second president of the United States. If you've ever had to memorize my name for a test, I'm truly sorry. That's not what I had in mind when I ran for office. It's nice to be remembered—*sure!*—but nobody likes to be a person you're *forced* to remember. It's just embarrassing!

Anyway, I come to these pages today not as a celebrity president, and not as the father of a semi-famous president, but as a proud grandfather with a special blowout offer on a genuine, limited-edition American collectible.

Have you heard of my grandson, CHARLES FRANCIS ADAMS (son of John Quincy Adams)?

As President Lincoln's ambassador to Britain during the Civil War, Chas Adams—my little-known grandson—kept the British from siding with the Confederates. (No small feat! Some of those Brits were still sore about losing the Revolutionary War.) Charles's diplomatic efforts to keep Britain neutral saved countless American lives and helped cement the Union victory.

Patriots everywhere agree—CHARLES FRANCIS ADAMS, the "Third Great Adams," deserves a home in our memory and a home on our fireplace mantels. That's why I'm offering this collectible CHARLES FRANCIS ADAMS MEMORIAL STATUETTE for the low price of $109.95.

Act now—supply limited.

John Adams

1:3 SCALE

P.S.

That severe-looking gentleman to the right is my son, John Quincy Adams, sixth president of the United States and father of my heroic grandson, CHARLES FRANCIS ADAMS.

Even though Charles didn't become a president, I like to think John Quincy was proud. After all, Charles helped persuade Britain to stop building warships for the Confederacy during the Civil War—no small feat! One British-built Confederate ship, the *Alabama*, stole over $6,000,000 in Union goods before it was destroyed.

My collectible sticker set—C. F. ADAMS AND DAD KEEPSAKE STICKERS—offers a distinctive visual tour through Charles's life. Once thought to be sold out, a few sets are still available. $39.95 per sheet.

INDEX TO THE STICKER COLLECTION

1. **HARVARD UNIVERSITY**—Charles Francis Adams studied here, and was later offered presidency of the university. He declined it.

2. **DANIEL WEBSTER**—Famed American attorney and two-time Secretary of State under whom Charles Francis Adams studied law.

3. **FURIOUS GORILLA BREAKING PENCIL**—This is what it probably felt like, sometimes, to be the son and grandson of U.S. presidents.

4. **ANDREW JACKSON**—Took the U.S. presidency from John Quincy Adams in the heated 1828 election. A family nemesis.

5. **1848 PRESIDENTIAL CAMPAIGN POSTER**—Charles Francis Adams was Martin Van Buren's running mate in an unsuccessful White House bid.

6. **BIRKENHEAD IRONWORKS, ENGLAND**—During the Civil War, Charles Francis Adams's heroic efforts helped to end its construction of massive, havoc-wreaking Confederate ships.

7. **THE HANDSHAKE**—Indispensible tool of diplomacy.

8. **JOHN QUINCY ADAMS PRESIDENTIAL LIBRARY**—Built by Charles Francis Adams in 1870 in Quincy, Massachusetts to house his father's presidential paraphernalia. It was the very first presidential library.

1. 2. 3. 4.

5. 6. 7. 8.

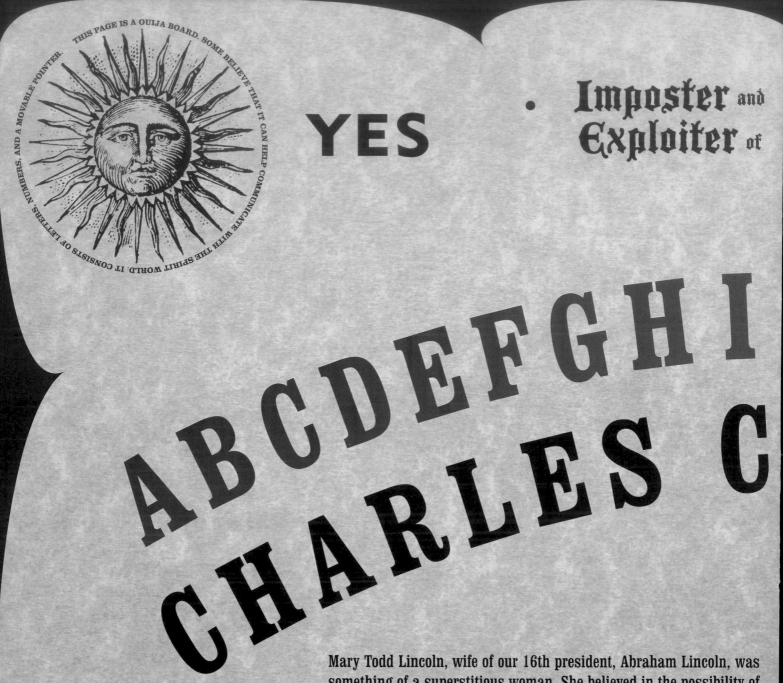

THIS PAGE IS A OUIJA BOARD. SOME BELIEVE THAT IT CAN HELP COMMUNICATE WITH THE SPIRIT WORLD. IT CONSISTS OF LETTERS, NUMBERS, AND A MOVABLE POINTER.

YES

. Imposter and Exploiter of

A B C D E F G H I

CHARLES C

Mary Todd Lincoln, wife of our 16th president, Abraham Lincoln, was something of a superstitious woman. She believed in the possibility of communicating with the dead, and would perhaps have put stock in a ouija board like this one. Unfortunately, there were those who took advantage of Mary's beliefs.

Charles Colchester was one such villain. After the death of the Lincolns' son Willie in 1862, Mrs. Lincoln was overcome with grief. Colchester presented himself as the solution, someone who could help Mary Todd speak with her dead son.

Colchester claimed to be a spiritual medium, and one evening he

FARE

Mary Todd Lincoln .

NO

JKLMNOPQR
OLCHESTER

convinced Mary Todd that he was delivering messages from Willie.

But Noah Brooks, a journalist and friend of the Lincolns, was skeptical. At a gathering being held to demonstrate Colchester's abilities, Brooks exposed him as a trickster and a fraud. Soon after, Colchester would attempt to blackmail Mrs. Lincoln, telling her that if she did not grant him a favor, he would deliver unfavorable news from the afterlife.

At Mrs. Lincoln's request, Brooks came to the White House to meet Colchester. Now face to face with his accuser, Colchester crumbled, left the White House, and fled Washington, never to be heard from by the Lincolns or Brooks again.

WELL

"PHONO

Hello, my name is F.B. Fenby, and I'm responsible for the **phonograph**.

After all, I did come up with the world's first sound recording device…

right?

Whenever you pop a CD in, or play an MP3, or whatever it is you youngsters are doing these days, you've got me to thank.

You see, in 1863, I patented the design for "The Electro-Magnetic Phonograph." The idea was that the machine would record keyboard strokes onto a piece of paper tape that could then be played back. Player pianos (the kind that play music on their own) use the same idea.

GRAPH"

Nice. Then it's settled. I did it. I invented the phonograph and I am responsible for all recorded music that followed thereafter.

Years later, Herman's company would join with three others to create the computer company IBM!

Herman Hollerith

early punch card device

what's that?

Thomas who?

Thomas Edison

Okay, I admit I was never able to build a model of my device, and for that reason Thomas Edison gets the credit for building the first working phonograph. But hey! I coined the name, and I did try. Edison, like every great inventor, built on the failed efforts of those before him, and I think I can be counted among those. Plus, my idea to punch holes in paper wasn't a complete failure! A man named Herman Hollerith later used punch cards in an invention that would lead to the modern computer!

Edison's phonograph

player piano rolls

CHRISTOPHER SHOLES

Newspaperman, Inventor, Hero

Gettin' Flirty with QWERTY

The Man, The Myth, the (Typewriting) Machine

Christopher Sholes

It's one of those mysteries you always wonder about, but never quite get around to looking into. At first, you think about it every time you look down from an email or a book report you're typing. Then, as time goes by, you just stop noticing. Here's the question:

Why in the world is a keyboard set up the way it is?!

A is next to S, which is next to D, F, G, H, J, K, and L, which are sort of in alphabetical order.

But then Z is next to X and C and V and B?

Why? Why in the World?

NOTE BOOK

Q.W.E.R.T.Y.

CHRISTOPHER SHOLES
The Down and Dirty on QWERTY

There's a man behind your keyboard and his name is Christopher Sholes.

Born on Valentine's Day in 1819, Sholes was seemingly destined to do what he did. Sholes's father trained him and his three brothers to be printers. At the age of eighteen, Sholes went to work for two of his older brothers who were publishing a newspaper in Green Bay, Wisconsin. Three years later, he founded his own weekly paper in Southport, Wisconsin. Christopher Sholes was born into printing and newspapers, and he would spend his whole life dedicated to them. But it would be many years before Sholes made his longest lasting contribution to the written word.

In 1867, Sholes was living in Milwaukee. He began working in a machine shop with an amateur inventor named Carlos Glidden. The two of them took an interest in typing machines, and while they weren't the first to do so, they made a working model that sparked some interest with other inventors. Sholes's early success with typewriters led him to continue tinkering. He started developing different models, and each time he would adjust the layout of the keyboard. He found that he had to spread certain letters out so that they wouldn't jam the keyboard when pressed one after the other. Finally, he settled on the arrangement we have today. The first six letters on the top row spell out the peculiar word QWERTY, and the layout has come to be referred to by that cute little name ever since.

Computers don't have the same problem of getting jammed like typewriters, but QWERTY has stuck around—even though a number of people have tried to develop better layouts. So even though it doesn't make sense, and it might not be the best, QWERTY is here to stay!

WAIT... ARE YOU CALLING ME A HERO OR A VILLAIN?!? THE FACT THAT SOME PEOPLE THINK THAT QWERTY IS A LITTLE QWERKY (KEYBOARD HUMOR!), SHOULDN'T TAKE AWAY FROM THE FACT THAT I CAME UP WITH A SYSTEM THAT HAS LASTED FOR A VERY, VERY LONG TIME!

Edmund McIlhenny

Was he a Saint...

INVENTOR OF ONE OF THE MOST POPULAR BRANDS OF HOT SAUCE ON THE PLANET. A TRUE FRIEND TO EGGS, SOUP, OYSTERS, AND SOMETIMES PIZZA.

Take a seat at just about any diner counter in America, and chances are you'll find yourself face to face with Edmund McIlhenny's pride and joy. Now, in order to fully immerse oneself in the glory of McIlhenny's contribution, you have to take a whiff. Or better yet, a taste. Spicy, huh? Well, to experience the salty burn of McIlhenny's Tabasco sauce is to taste a little bit of Americana (and a whole lot of peppers).

During the Civil War, the tiny Louisiana territory of Avery Island served a small but important function. Salt was vital to preserving food back then, and Avery Island had an abundance of it. Edmund McIlhenny, a devout lover of food, chose Avery Island as the perfect place to experiment with some pepper seeds a friend had brought him from Mexico. After the Civil War, Edmund combined his peppers with the natural salt found on Avery Island to create an elixir that quickly became a favorite of innumerable heat-seeking diners.

What else is Tabasco good for? Well, at various times, it has been thought to cure disease, used to polish brass on Navy ships, and wielded as a weapon to ward off intruders. Of course, these days it's mostly just used to add a little kick to bland food. So creating one of the world's most popular condiments should certainly qualify Edmund McIlhenny as a hero, right? Well wait just a second. Turn the page and read on!

...OR A SCOURGE?!

THE NUTRIA RAT. VERMIN WITHOUT REMORSE. PLAGUE OF THE SOUTH. DID EDMUND MCILHENNY, TABASCO KING, UNLEASH THIS ANIMAL UPON OUR UNSUSPECTING COUNTRY?

Throughout marsh-like areas in the United States—specifically in states like Louisiana, Florida, Oregon, and Maryland—a dog-sized rodent known as a nutria wreaks havoc on the environment. It burrows rapidly and consumes vital plant roots at an alarming rate. Other animals are edged out of their habitats, and wetlands are destroyed in the process.

But the nutria isn't even native to the United States. How did it get here? For years, popular thought has held that Edmund McIlhenny, the hot sauce hero, introduced the nutria to the U.S. Looking to harvest the nutria's soft fur, he imported them from South America in the 1930s, and released many of them into the Louisiana wild. Can this be true? Was Edmund McIlhenny an evil mastermind whose aim was only to burn our tongues and ruin the South's natural beauty?

In recent years, word has surfaced that McIlhenny was not the first person to bring nutria into the United States. In fact, he bought his nutria from a farmer already raising them in Louisiana. Vindicated at last! Well, not really. The fact is, McIlhenny was still one of the first commercial farmers of nutria. He definitely did release the critters into the wild, and while not all the blame rests on his shoulders, Edmund definitely deserves some of it.

The lesson? Think about your actions. It's fine to make money, but don't set gigantic rats free in the process!

66

COPYRIGHT
1903
E. S. CURTIS

CHIEF JOSEPH

[or, Hin-mut-too-yah-lat-kekht (Thunder Rolling in Mountain)]

ONE OF THE GREAT LEADERS OF THE NEZ PERCE TRIBE OF NATIVE AMERICANS

the name
Nez Perce
is actually a misnomer.

The Nez Perce tribe originally called itself Nimi'ipuu. The name Nez Perce was assigned to them by French traders, who saw that some tribe members had pierced noses (nez percé), and thus named the tribe after this somewhat isolated practice.

BORN AROUND 1840, JOSEPH WAS THE SON OF ANOTHER GREAT NEZ PERCE CHIEF NAMED TUEKAKAS, FROM WHOM HE INHERITED A DECADES-LONG STRUGGLE TO FIND PEACE WITH ENCROACHING SETTLERS

Unfortunately, this was ultimately a struggle that would prove to be too difficult to win.

The proud tribes native to America would be overrun by pioneers eager for more land.

It's our duty to remember and respect their place as the native people of this country.

YEARS OF FIGHTING FOR THE RIGHT TO LIVE ON THEIR OWN ANCESTRAL LAND TOOK THEIR TOLL ON THE NEZ PERCE, AND IN 1877, AFTER ONE FINAL ATTEMPT TO DEFEND THEMSELVES A tired Chief Joseph FAMOUSLY PROCLAIMED –

THEY LIVED IN PARTS OF MODERN-DAY WASHINGTON, OREGON, & IDAHO

FROM WHERE *the* SUN NOW STANDS, I WILL FIGHT NO MORE FOREVER.

OFFICIAL BALLOT

CONSOLIDATED GENERAL ELECTION

NOVEMBER 5, 1872

INSTRUCTIONS TO VOTERS: Complete the arrow pointing to your choice, as shown in the picture. To vote for a qualified write-in candidate, write the person's name on the blank line provided and complete the arrow.

THIS IS NOT REALLY AN OFFICIAL BALLOT: Obviously, right? It's in a book. Still, this is what a ballot looks like in many instances. What we'd like to draw your attention to is the third candidate for president: Victoria Woodhull.

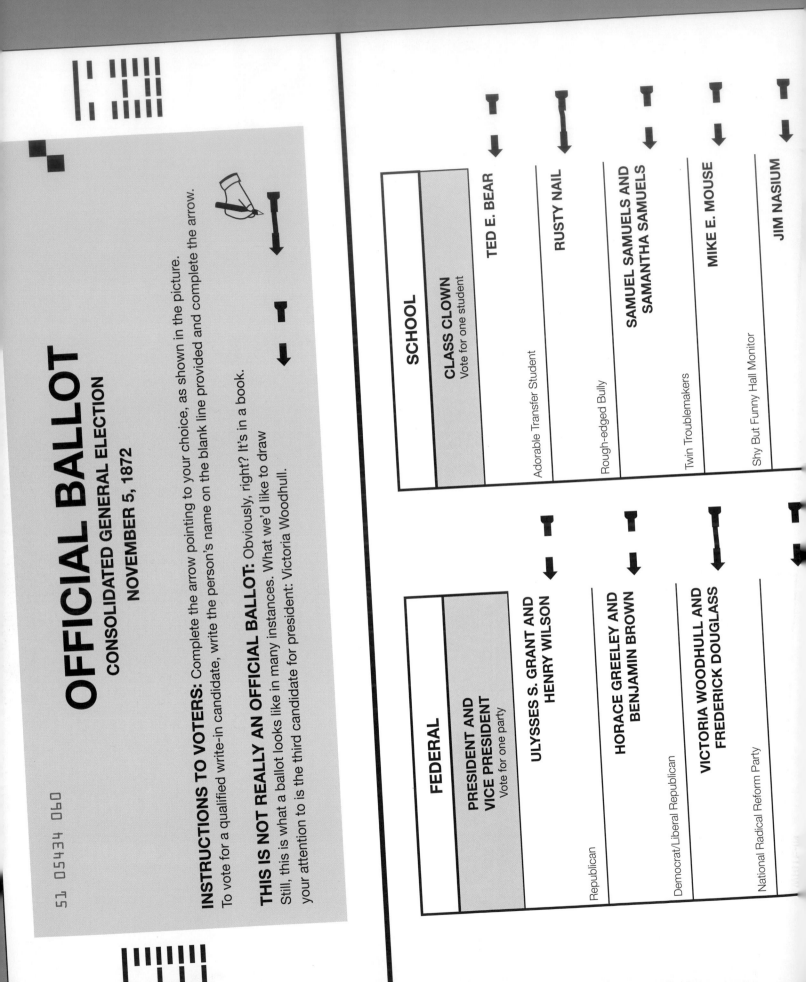

FEDERAL

PRESIDENT AND VICE PRESIDENT
Vote for one party

ULYSSES S. GRANT AND HENRY WILSON

Republican

HORACE GREELEY AND BENJAMIN BROWN

Democrat/Liberal Republican

VICTORIA WOODHULL AND FREDERICK DOUGLASS

National Radical Reform Party

SCHOOL

CLASS CLOWN
Vote for one student

TED E. BEAR

Adorable Transfer Student

RUSTY NAIL

Rough-edged Bully

SAMUEL SAMUELS AND SAMANTHA SAMUELS

Twin Troublemakers

MIKE E. MOUSE

Shy But Funny Hall Monitor

JIM NASIUM

VICTORIA WOODHULL

...was the first woman to be nominated for President of the United States. Born on September 23, 1838, Victoria was one of ten brothers and sisters. Her mother Roxanna and father Reuben ran a traveling show, which featured fortune-telling and other spiritualist acts. Woodhull and her sister Tennessee Claflin worked with their parents for some time before striking out on their own. Together they started a stock brokerage company and achieved a good deal of success. They used the profits from the company to found their own newspaper, *Woodhull and Claflin's Weekly*. Through the newspaper they voiced their strong opinions on women's rights, specifically on women's suffrage (the right to vote).

In April of 1870, Victoria shocked the nation when she announced in a letter to the *New York Herald* that she would seek the presidency of the United States. She was running as the candidate of the National Radical Reform Party. Her choice for a running mate was quite intriguing, too. As vice-presidential nominee, she chose the outspoken abolitionist leader and former slave Frederick Douglass. The Douglass and Woodhull ticket captured only a tiny portion of the national vote, but their campaign has great symbolic meaning.

Today, 140 years later, we still have not had a female president or vice president. Senator Hillary Clinton came close to getting a Democratic presidential nomination in 2008, but lost to Barack Obama. Obama, meanwhile, went on to become our country's first African-American President, a great step toward breaking down social barriers in the U.S.!

WRITE-IN

STATE

UNITED STATES SENATE
Vote for one

ORRIS S. FERRY

Liberal Republican

CLASS PRESIDENT AND VICE PRESIDENT
Vote for one party

GEORGE SHRUB AND RICHARD RAIMI

Junior Libertarians

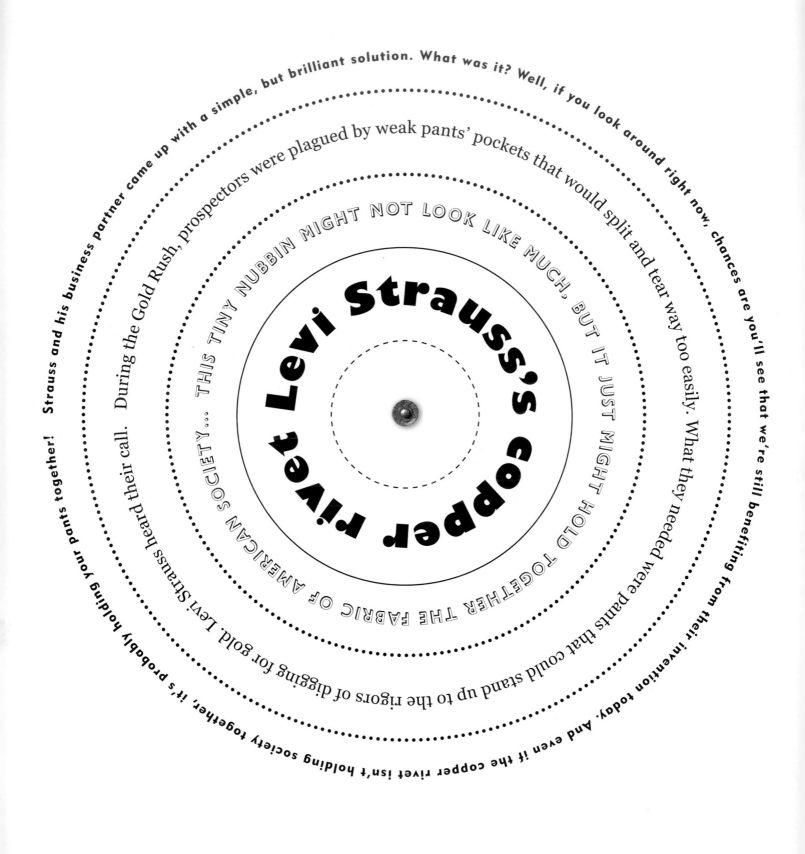

Levi Strauss's copper rivet

THIS TINY NUBBIN MIGHT NOT LOOK LIKE MUCH, BUT IT JUST MIGHT HOLD TOGETHER THE FABRIC OF AMERICAN SOCIETY...

During the Gold Rush, prospectors were plagued by weak pants' pockets that would split and tear way too easily. What they needed were pants that could stand up to the rigors of digging for gold. Levi Strauss heard their call.

Strauss and his business partner came up with a simple, but brilliant solution. What was it? Well, if you look around right now, chances are you'll see that we're still benefiting from their invention today. And even if the copper rivet isn't holding society together, it's probably holding your pants together!

LEVI STRAUSS AND THE COPPER RIVET

(THE STORY OF A SMALL METAL STUD)

(1) Levi Strauss, born in Bavaria, emigrated to New York as a sixteen-year-old with his mother and siblings.

(2) In 1853, Strauss became an American citizen and traveled to San Francisco, eager to capitalize on the Gold Rush.

(3) In San Francisco, Levi found success as a merchant, selling goods and clothing to fortune-seeking gold miners.

(4) In 1872, Levi met Jacob Davis, a tailor from Nevada, who began making pants out of denim he bought from Levi. In order to strengthen the pockets, he was fastening them with metal rivets. But Davis didn't have the money to patent his idea, so he appealed to Levi for assistance. Levi knew a good idea when he saw one, and in 1873, the blue jean was born.

THE GREATEST TAIL ON EARTH

JUMBO THE ELEPHANT

THE BIGGEST
ELEPHANT
IN THE WORLD

ACCORDING TO P.T. BARNUM,
WORLD-FAMOUS SHOWMAN &
PURVEYOR OF GENERAL AMUSEMENTS,
INCLUDING THE SELF-PROCLAIMED
GREATEST SHOW ON EARTH

• BORN IN 1861 IN ETHIOPIA • SUFFERED AN UNTIMELY DEATH AT THE MERCY OF A FREIGHT TRAIN ON SEPTEMBER 15, 1885 IN CANADA •

• "JUMBO" •

OBTAINED IN SPITE OF THE VEHEMENT PROTESTS OF
THE PEOPLE AND GOVERNMENT OF GREAT BRITAIN...

A PACHYDERM UNLIKE ANY OTHER ON EARTH!

The star of London's Royal Zoological Society!

AN UNRIVALED APPETITE!

KNOWN TO CONSUME 200 POUNDS (90 KG) OF HAY, A BARREL OF POTATOES, 2 BUSHELS OF OATS, 15 LOAVES OF BREAD, PAILS UPON PAILS OF WATER, AND GALLONS OF WHISKEY

IN JUST A SINGLE DAY!

JUMBO CAPTURED THE HEARTS OF AMERICANS, CHANGING THE CIRCUS WORLD FOREVER AND CEMENTING HIS NAME IN AMERICAN LORE!

THE TOWERING MONARCH OF HIS MIGHTY RACE

COME ONE ★ COME ALL

HIS LEGACY BURNS BRIGHTLY

JUMBO TOURED THE COUNTRY EVEN AFTER HIS DEATH. AT LEAST, HIS STUFFED BODY DID. HIS NAME HAS SINCE BECOME SYNONYMOUS WITH

ENORMOUS.

JUMBO THE ELEPHANT

WAS A 6.5-TON AFRICAN ELEPHANT THAT TOURED THE WORLD FOR 4 GLORIOUS YEARS WITH THE CIRCUS BEFORE A MOST TRAGIC END,

KILLED BY A SPEEDING LOCOMOTIVE.

NELLIE BLY: NOT CRAZY!

Intrepid Reporter Feigns Insanity; Exposes Poor Conditions in Mental Institution

SHE ALSO TRAVELS AROUND THE WORLD IN RECORD TIME

THE NEW WORLD RECORD:
72 DAYS, 6 HOURS, 11 MINUTES

PLUS:

SHE INVENTED THE 55-GALLON STEEL DRUM

Bly Tells All in "Ten Days in a Mad-House"

Declared "Positively Demented," and Sent to Blackwell Island Insane Asylum, Bly Wrote a Book on the Deplorable Conditions and Abusive Doctors She Met.

In September 1887, Nellie Bly embarked upon a daring mission to discover what it was like to live in an insane asylum. Pretending to be a very confused woman, she managed to convince a judge and doctors that she was insane enough to be committed to an asylum.

At Blackwell Island, Bly joined hundreds of women—many of whom she found to be perfectly sane—being mistreated by an abusive staff, given cold baths, and fed inedible food. She stayed a total of 10 days before friends who knew of her mission secured her release.

After her release, Bly testified before a grand jury, and led a tour of the Blackwell facility. Despite the fact that the facility had gotten word of the visit and cleaned up their act, Bly convinced the jury of the plight of women at the asylum.

In the end, thanks to Bly's brave acts, the jury awarded more than $1 million to improving facilities for the mentally ill.

NELLIE BLY.
Defender of the weak, circumnavigator of the world.

A JOURNALISTIC PIONEER.

She dared to explore the places and topics that no one else would… or could.

Elizabeth Jane Cochrane was born on May 5, 1864, in Pennsylvania. By her teenage years, she was living a penniless existence. She left home for Pittsburgh to seek work as a journalist.

After reading an article titled, "What Girls are Good For," which described women's roles as being those of housekeepers and child-raisers, an infuriated Cochrane wrote a letter to the editor.

Impressed by her tenacity, the editor of the paper, the *Pittsburgh Dispatch*, hired Cochrane soon after.

Like many other women writers of the era, Cochrane adopted a pen name, and thus Nellie Bly was born, as was a new era for women journalists.

Bly went on to log several extraordinary feats during her storied career. She set a record by circling the Earth in only 72 days (besting the fictional record set forth by author Jules Verne), posed as a mental patient to uncover abuses by the staff of an asylum, and invented a steel barrel that became an industry standard.

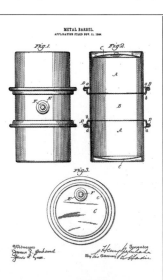

55-GALLON DRUM.
Revolutionized the oil industry.

INTREPID REPORTER SECURES PATENT FOR 55-GALLON DRUM

After Circling the World, Bly Impresses Again; This Time with Barrel.

In the early 20th century, oil companies were plagued by weak wooden barrels that were prone to leaking. In 1905, inspired by containers she had seen in Europe, Nellie Bly invented and patented the first durable steel oil drums in America. Bly's invention became the standard used by oil companies everywhere.

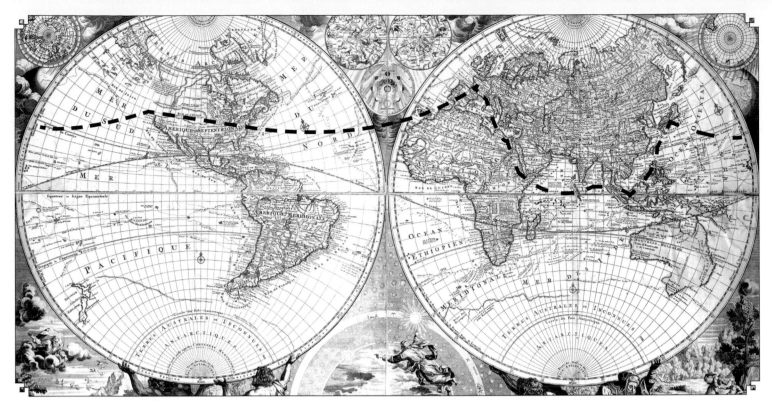

HER RECORD-SETTING JOURNEY.

Bly traveled from New York, to England, to France, to Italy, to Egypt, to Yemen, to Sri Lanka, to Malaysia, to Singapore, to Hong Kong, to Japan, to San Francisco, and back to New York.

Around the World in 72 Days with Nellie Bly

Inspired by Jules Verne's *Around the World In 80 Days*, Bly Set Out to Make History by Circling the Globe in record time.

On November 14, 1889, renowned reporter and brave soul Nellie Bly set sail from New York Harbor for London, England, aboard the steamship *Augusta Victoria*. This was to be the first leg of her groundbreaking trip around the world.

Her goal? To best the time set by fictional character Phileas Fogg in the novel *Around the World in 80 Days.*

A mere seventy-two days, six hours, and eleven minutes later, having passed through 11 countries and territories, Bly finally returned to New York City on January 25, 1890.

During her travels, Bly had the privilege of meeting with none other than Jules Verne, author of *Around the World in 80 Days*, at his home in Amiens, France. Verne wished Nellie luck on the journey ahead of her, and in her attempt to break Fogg's record.

From France, Bly traveled south to Italy, and then on to Egypt. The next leg of her journey took her through southern Asia, and back north to Hong Kong and Japan.

Whenever possible, Bly sent telegrams to her newspaper's office in New York. From these short messages, the editors of the paper created updates for a captivated public. Occasionally, when timing and the mail system would allow, Bly was able to treat audiences to longer pieces of her own.

All told, Bly traveled 21,740 miles (34,987 km). A majority of her travel was conducted by ship and train, but at several stops she ventured by more unusual means, including a jinrickshaw, sampan, sedan chair, bullock hackery, and gharry.

After crossing 18 bodies of water and purchasing one monkey, Bly set a new world record and ushered in a new era of global travel.

A SEDAN CHAIR.
That's not Nellie Bly, though.

HOW NELLIE GOT AROUND

JINRICKSHAW: A "small two-wheel wagon" with "shafts joined at the end with a crossbar," pulled by men wearing "little else than a sash."

SAMPAN: "An oddly shaped flat boat with the oars, or rather paddles, fastened near the stern. The Malay oarsman rowed hand over hand, standing upright."

BULLOCK HACKERY: A "very small springless cart on two wheels" pulled by a bullock, a "modest-looking little animal with a hump on its back and crooked horns on its head."

GHARRY: "A light wagon with latticed windows and comfortable seating room for four... drawn by a pretty spotted Malay pony whose speed is marvelous."

SEDAN CHAIR: A seat carried by men who "hoist the chair to their shoulders and start off with a monotonous trot."

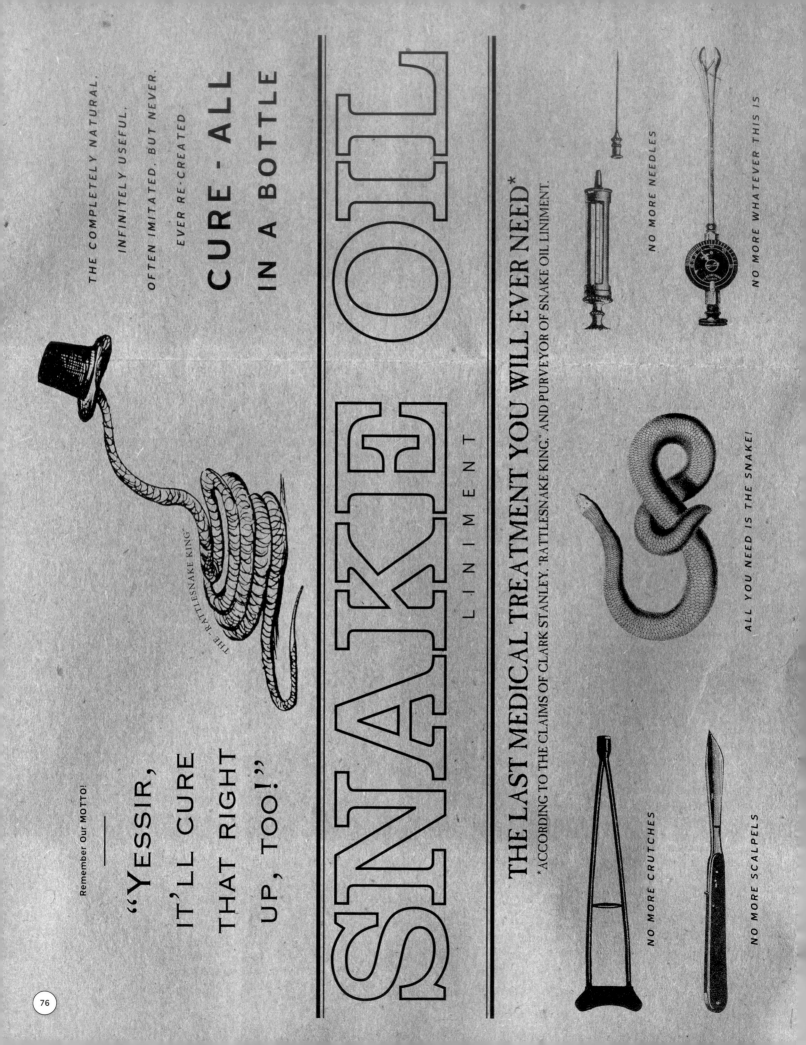

THE COMPLETELY NATURAL.

INFINITELY USEFUL.

OFTEN IMITATED. BUT NEVER.

EVER RE-CREATED

CURE - ALL

IN A BOTTLE

SNAKE OIL

LINIMENT

"THE 'RATTLESNAKE KING'"

Remember Our MOTTO!

"YESSIR,
IT'LL CURE
THAT RIGHT
UP, TOO!"

THE LAST MEDICAL TREATMENT YOU WILL EVER NEED*

*ACCORDING TO THE CLAIMS OF CLARK STANLEY, "RATTLESNAKE KING," AND PURVEYOR OF SNAKE OIL LINIMENT.

NO MORE NEEDLES

NO MORE WHATEVER THIS IS

ALL YOU NEED IS THE SNAKE!

NO MORE CRUTCHES

NO MORE SCALPELS

76

WHAT THE SNAKE CAN (OR CAN'T) DO FOR YOU

HISTORY. Clark Stanley was born in Abilene, Texas around the time of the Civil War. For much of his youth, he was an outdoorsman, a cowboy. In 1879, his father's friends brought him along on a trip to witness the snake dance of the Moki Indians in Arizona.

According to Stanley, he stayed with the tribe for more than two years, and learned a great deal from the tribe, especially their medicine man. Of special interest to Stanley was snake oil, a medicine (derived from snakes, of course) that the tribe had used "for many generations." When he returned from his trip, Stanley began to tell people that he had "improved" the formula for snake oil, and in doing so, had found a cure to numerous ailments.

CLAIMS. Stanley began showing off his new invention. Once, in 1893, at The World's Columbian Exhibition in Chicago, Stanley even created the potion in front of a live audience. He grabbed live snakes, killed them, extracted the snake "oil," and mixed it with other ingredients. He would claim then, and in numerous ads that looked like this page, that his snake oil (or Snake Oil Liniment, as he called it) could treat anything from headaches, to bug bites, to bruises, to paralysis.

VILLAINY. Of course, many if not all of Stanley's claims were exaggerated or downright made up. Snake oil can't really cure paralysis, or sciatica, or sprains. Most of the stuff in Snake Oil Liniment wasn't really from snakes, anyway. But Stanley's act was not unique. Numerous people before him and after him have tried to convince the public that their potions and pills can cure all sorts of diseases or make you better looking. Snake Oil Liniment was just one among many!

CONSEQUENCE. Even though Stanley's creation was one of many such fake medications, his has the undignified honor of representing all of them. The term "snake oil," now refers to anything that someone tries to sell you and pass off as a cure-all. Let that be a lesson to you! Try to cheat people, and your name will go down in history (and not in a good way).

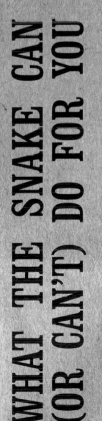

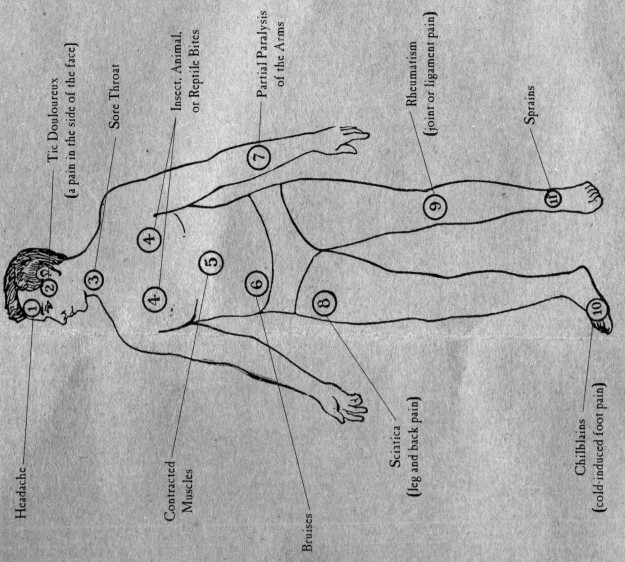

Headache

Tic Douloureux (a pain in the side of the face)

Sore Throat

Insect, Animal, or Reptile Bites

Partial Paralysis of the Arms

Rheumatism (joint or ligament pain)

Sprains

Contracted Muscles

Bruises

Sciatica (leg and back pain)

Chilblains (cold-induced foot pain)

Figure 1. Some of the numerous ailments curable by snake oil liniment, as claimed by Clark Stanley

JOHN HARVEY KELLOGG

The Cereal Flake Co-Creator who was, Himself, a Tad Flaky

 In 1876, Dr. John Harvey Kellogg founded the Battle Creek Sanitarium, a popular retreat in Michigan for people suffering from exhaustion and other health problems. Visitors to "The San" included rich and famous Americans like car baron Henry Ford and President Warren G. Harding.

Kellogg was a Seventh-Day Adventist and a staunch vegetarian. He enforced a strict diet at the San: visitors could drink no tea, coffee, cocoa, or cocktails, and they weren't allowed to smoke. Kellogg also called for lots of exercise and enemas (plural—as in many enemas per visit. Yikes!). This rough regimen was all part of what Kellogg called "biologic living."

Unfortunately, most of the food tasted horrible. Also: Kellogg insisted that everyone chew the food many, many times. That sounds pretty terrible, right?

Adventures in Health Food

Rewind a few years. In 1863, a man named James Jackson had invented Granula—the first cold breakfast cereal. (It was nuggety like Grape-Nuts, only harder.) Kellogg loved Granula, so he decided to made his own version, also called Granula. When Dr. Jackson got word of this copycatting, he sued Kellogg. Then Kellogg changed the name of his product to Granola.

Always on the hunt for new nutritious foods, Kellogg experimented with all kinds of seeds, nuts, and grains. His numerous nut creations include "Protose" a peanut-based meat substitute that tasted (supposedly) like chicken *and* beef. Weird.

The Corn Flake and the Competitor

In the 1890s, John Harvey Kellogg and his younger brother, Will Keith Kellogg, invented the process of "flaking" grains by crushing and baking them. "Granose Flakes" (wheat) came first, and corn flakes followed. Meanwhile, a San patient named Charles Post took notes on the Kellogg menu. He created Grape-Nuts in 1897 and marketed it all around the country. By 1900, Post was rich. Will thought he and his brother

EUGENICS

EUGENICS IS THE SELF DIRECTION

OF HUMAN EVOLUTION

LIKE A TREE
EUGENICS DRAWS ITS MATERIALS FROM MANY SOURCES AND ORGANIZES
THEM INTO AN HARMONIOUS ENTITY.

should spend more time advertising and selling their cereals at grocery stores like Post did, but John disagreed. He wanted to stay focused on being a doctor.

In 1906, the brothers argued and parted ways after John caught Will adding sugar cane to the corn flakes to make them taste better.

After the falling out, Will Keith started his own cereal company, which thrived, and eventually become the Kellogg Company—the biggest cereal company in the world. Meanwhile, John Harvey continued his nutritional and medical work, and developing improved instruments and performing surgeries into his seventies.

The Not-So-Heroic Part

Although John Harvey Kellogg helped to define America's understanding of the "healthy lifestyle," he was also a prominent eugenicist—someone who aims to develop a superior race of humans through controlled breeding. In 1906, Kellogg co-founded the Race Betterment Foundation, which was intent on creating a new race of white "thoroughbreds."

Still, Kellogg was not some simple monster. He and his wife generously cared for dozens of orphaned children—both white and non-white—all their lives.

John Harvey Kellogg had hoped to live to 100, but died of pneumonia at age 91.

PROTOSE

— PEANUT–BASED MEAT SUBSTITUTE —

FOR A TASTE NOT UNLIKE CHICKEN

SEVENTH-DAY ADVENTIST ?

Come worship each Saturday with John Harvey Kellogg and others of us who choose to observe the Sabbath one day before most people do. Founded in Battle Creek, MI in 1863, our Church uniquely emphasizes faith, diet, and health in a fashion that has led to our worldwide growth.

CORN: "HERO OF ITS OWN STORY"?

A seer named Michael Pollan reports o[n] dominant role corn will play in the [ ] of this country: "Though we hu[ ] [will soon play] a crucial ro[le] corn's rise to world domin[ ] it would be wrong to su[ ] we [will be] calling t[he] shots, or acting [ ] always in our ow[n] best interests. Indeed, there i[s] every reason [to] believe that [ ] corn will [ ] succeed in [ ] domestica[ting] us." Bless [ ] the warni[ng] Brother [ ] we have [ ]

FORGET [ME]AT?

[ ]GOT [ ]MS.

CAT[ ] B[ ] CH[ ]

BUY OUR STO[VE]

CAST IRON STOVET[ ] [AVAI]LABLE F[OR] SALES SEND POS[T] OKALAHOMA C[ ] BEAUTIFUL A[ ] [T]O YOUR KITCHEN. 10[ ]

[ ]LOGIC LIVING

12 Niday St., Bat C[ ]

Oops.

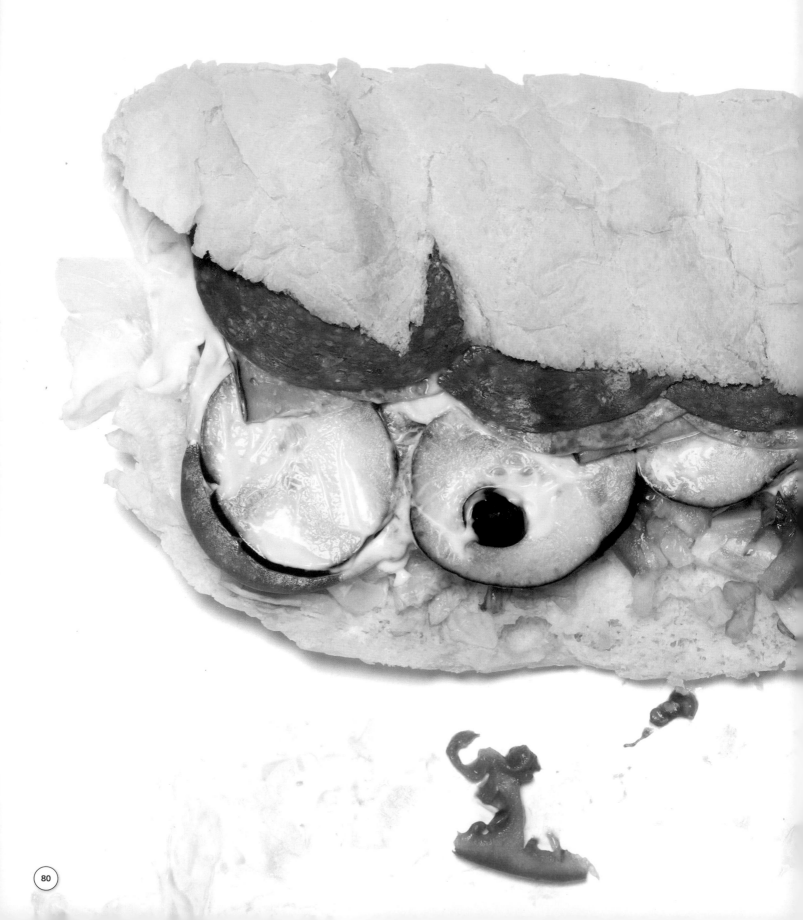

We meant to hide this delicious hero sandwich in a corner of our nasty office mini-fridge, but we accidentally filed it here on pages 80 and 81 instead. Sorry. (I guess that's what happens when you come to work without getting enough sleep.) Anyway, if you didn't grow up in New York, you might prefer to call this poor smashed sandwich by one of its many other regional and commercial names: *hoagie*, *sub*, *submarine*, *torpedo*, *grinder*, *poor boy*, *po' boy*, *Italian sandwich*, *rocket*, *zeppelin*, *zep*, *garibaldi*, *blimpie*, *spuckie*, *bomber*, *wedge*, and *muffuletta*. All of these sandwiches share a basic formula: a large bread roll filled with a variety of sliced meats and cheeses, plus tomato, lettuce, and onion (or other veggies), and maybe a sprinkle of oil and spices.

The term "hero" for a sandwich like this is often attributed to Clementine Paddleford, a food columnist for the *New York Herald Tribune*. In the 1930s, Paddleford supposedly wrote that the sandwich was so large, "you had to be a hero to eat it." But enthusiastic sandwich historians have recently concluded that Paddleford never wrote that. Instead, they say, the term "hero sandwich" dates to 1947, and they say it will probably remain the preferred term among a few hungry New Yorkers forever.

Whatever you call it, the hero sandwich was popularized by Italian–Americans in the northeastern U.S. during the late nineteenth century. Now if you'll excuse me, I gotta eat this thing before it gets messed up worse.

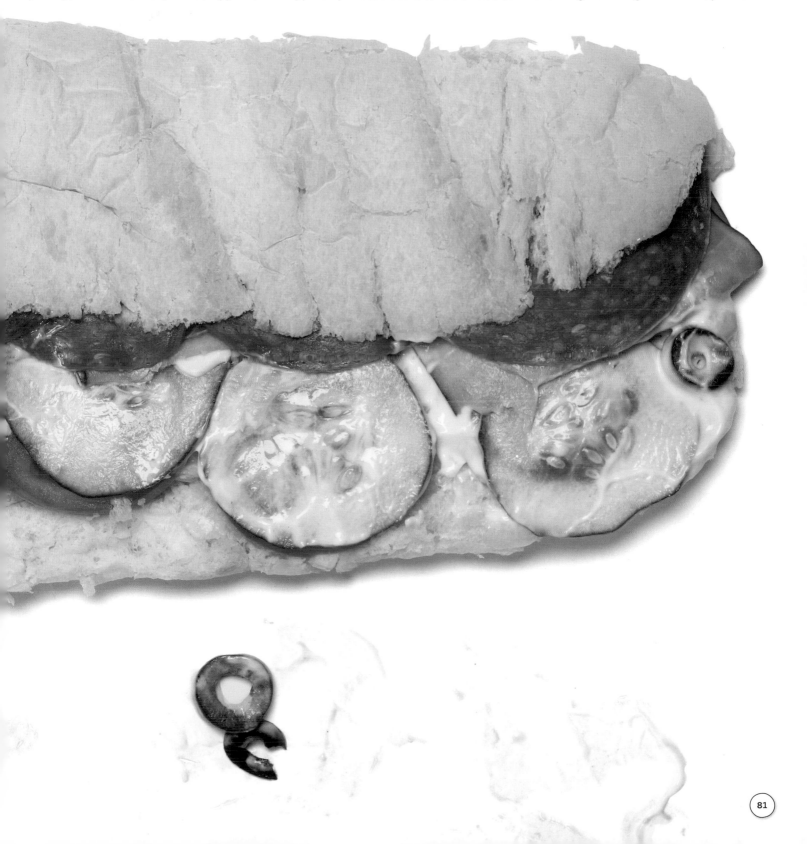

HUGO

PA WILL BE KILLED IT'S UP TO ME

HER

World's First Comics Superhero?

On September 7, 1902, readers of *The Chicago Sunday Tribune*'s new Comics Supplement were introduced to Hugo Hercules, the first gallant and benevolent* superhuman to appear in comics.

The mild-mannered Hugo would wander around Chicago doing things like catching a falling safe, pulling a stalled locomotive along its tracks, and wrestling a runaway cart-horse into submission. One super-heroic act per week.

Although "Hugo Hercules" was a somewhat popular strip—it sometimes received the top slot in the Supplement—it ended just months after it began, when its creator, William H.D. Koerner, decided to give up comics and seek fame and fortune as a painter in New York City.

Thirty-six years before Superman landed on newsstands, 32 years before the invention of the modern comic book, 27 years before Popeye first ate spinach, and 15 years before the word *superhero* was ever recorded in a dictionary, Hugo Hercules stood as comics' first embodiment of that thoroughly American (and totally comic-booky) character type: the superhero.

* So Hugo accepts a little cash reward sometimes. Does that make him less *heroic*? Less *benevolent*? Nope! On the contrary, in fact. That almost-killed man in panel 3 *wants* to pay Hugo. Why deny him the pleasure?

1. TOO CUTE TO SHOOT

IN NOVEMBER OF 1902, THE 26TH PRESIDENT OF THE UNITED STATES, THEODORE ROOSEVELT, WENT ON A GROUP HUNTING TRIP IN MISSISSIPPI. ONE OF HIS COMPANIONS CAUGHT A BLACK BEAR CUB AND PRESENTED IT TO THE PRESIDENT AS AN EASY TARGET. ROOSEVELT, PERHAPS HYPNOTIZED BY THE CUTE FACE OF THE TRAPPED CUB, TURNED DOWN THE OFFER. WHAT'S THE POINT OF SHOOTING AN ALREADY-TRAPPED BEAR?

CHUBBY BELLY IMPLIES SPECIMEN IS A WELL-FED, HEALTHY BEAR

WELL-ROUNDED BOTTOM PROVIDES STRUCTURAL STABILITY AND IMPROVED CUDDLY-WUDDLINESS.

SOFT, PADDED FEET STAND IN FOR ACTUAL TERRIBLE, VIOLENT CLAWS

2. WORD TRAVELS FAST

A REPORTER WAS ALONG FOR THE TRIP. HE TELEGRAPHED THE STORY BACK TO THE WASHINGTON POST, WHICH RAN A CARTOON BY A MAN NAMED CLIFFORD BERRYMAN. THE TOON PORTRAYED THE SCENE WITH THE BEAR CUB, AND THE WORDS: "DRAWING THE LINE IN MISSISSIPPI."

DATE	DETAILED BLUEPRINTS FOR A	
1902	TEDDY BEAR	Teddy Roosevelt's Industrial Design, LLC. *Putting the Teddy in Teddy Bear since 1902*

3. TEDDY'S BEAR

WHEN MORRIS MICHTOM OF BROOKLYN, NEW YORK SAW THE CARTOON, HE WAS INSPIRED. HE'D ALREADY BEEN TRYING TO SELL SOME TOY BEARS THAT HIS WIFE MADE, AND THIS CARTOON PROVIDED THE PERFECT SALES BOOSTER. MICHTOM WROTE TO THE WHITE HOUSE, ASKING FOR PERMISSION TO USE ROOSEVELT'S NAME. PERMISSION WAS GRANTED, AND MICHTOM STARTED SELLING "TEDDY'S BEARS" IN HIS NEW YORK STORE.

4. A TOY FIT FOR A PRESIDENT

TEDDY'S BEARS TOOK OFF IN POPULARITY, AND THE NAME WAS EVENTUALLY SHORTENED TO THE FAMILIAR "TEDDY BEARS."

SO WHILE HE DIDN'T INVENT THE BEARS, OR SEW THEM, OR PROBABLY EVEN OWN ONE, WITHOUT TEDDY ROOSEVELT, THE CLASSIC AMERICAN TEDDY BEAR JUST WOULDN'T BE A TEDDY BEAR.

SIMPLE BEADY EYES REDUCE THE TERROR THAT A REAL BEAR CAN CAUSE IN A SMALL CHILD.

THE WORLD'S LARGEST TEDDY BEAR WAS BUILT BY DANA WARREN OF OKLAHOMA. IT'S 55 FEET (16.8 M) TALL (THE BEAR, NOT MS. WARREN).

55 FEET

WHAT'S INSIDE A TEDDY BEAR? COTTON, PROBABLY. STILL, FEW PEOPLE ARE WILLING TO TEAR OPEN A TEDDY BEAR TO GET A PEEK AT THE TRUTH INSIDE, SO THERE'S A CHANCE THAT THE BEARS ARE FULL OF MARSHMALLOWS. LIKE THESE:

DUKE KAHANAMOKU

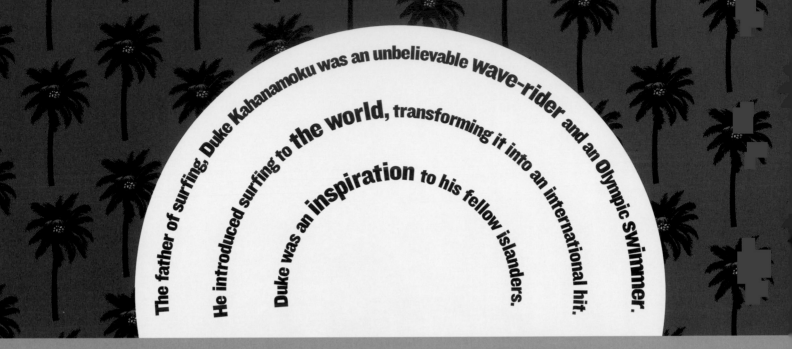

The father of surfing, Duke Kahanamoku was an unbelievable wave-rider and an Olympic swimmer.

He introduced surfing to the world, transforming it into an international hit.

Duke was an inspiration to his fellow islanders.

Duke Paoa Kahinu Mokoe Hulikohola Kahanamoku

was born on the big island of Honolulu, Hawaii in 1890— a turbulent time in the island's history. A century of exploitation at the hands of explorers and businessmen had left the native Hawaiian population decimated. And while Duke came from a relatively privileged family, he would never forget his role as a proud son of Hawaii and as a cultural ambassador for the islands.

From an early age, Kahanamoku demonstrated some pretty impressive skills in the water. Duke was an unbelievably speedy swimmer. While competing at an Amateur Athletic Union event when he was 21, he bested the previous 100-yard freestyle world record by nearly five seconds. The judges didn't believe it. They measured the course four times before finally admitting that Duke was really just that good.

At the 1912 Olympic Games, Duke won two swimming gold medals. In 1920 (the 1916 games were cancelled because of World War I), he won another two. Then he won a silver medal in his last Olympic Games in 1924.

Surfing

had yet to reach most places by the time Duke became an Olympic star. But Duke used his newfound swimming celebrity to promote the sport. He gave surfing demonstrations in the United States and in Australia. Surfing took off after that, and thus Duke has come to be considered the father of modern surfing.

If that's not impressive enough, an incident on June 14, 1925, should lock up Duke's place in the history books. On that day, off the coast of California, a small boat capsized, leaving 29 passengers floundering in the water. Duke immediately jumped onto his surfboard and paddled out to the scene. Using his board, he helped with the rescue effort, ferrying eight passengers to safety.

Duke was later appointed Hawaii's official greeter in recognition of all he had done to bring attention to the state. He was inducted into both the Swimming Hall of Fame and the Surfing Hall of Fame.

Without Duke Kahanamoku, surfing may never have reached the audience it has today. People would just be flailing around in the water, never knowing the thrill of having a board under their feet, cruising atop the face of the ocean.

CARL G. FISHER

Dreamed and built

THE LINCOLN
HIGHWAY

The first road across the United States

By 1910, almost 200,000 cars were in use in the United States. But the roads were terrible!

Most roads were just dirt, with deep ruts that could stop you in your tracks. And a lot of the roads didn't lead anywhere useful. Drivers had to constantly stop and ask for directions. Most people had no idea what happened to the roads 15 miles or so from where they lived.

Carl G. Fisher set out to change all that.

In September 1912, Fisher—a successful car dealer from Indianapolis—held a big dinner party for people involved in the automobile business and explained his grand plan for a road that would stretch clear across the United States. "Let's build it before we're too old to enjoy it!" he exclaimed.

Fisher estimated that for $10 million, they could create a reliable gravel highway from coast to coast. His goal was to finish the highway—starting in New York and ending in San Francisco—in two and a half years. The federal government didn't pay for road-building in those days, so Fisher had to raise the money on his own. Just a half hour after Fisher made his rousing speech, Frank Seiberling—founder of Goodyear tires—wrote a check for $300,000.

Within a few months, Fisher had raised over a million dollars, and newspapers around the country were covering the project. The president of Packard Motor Car Company, Henry Joy, sent along $150,000 and encouraged Fisher to dedicate the road to his hero—Abraham Lincoln. (He did.)

Six years and $25 million later, the dream was a reality. The Lincoln Highway was dedicated in 1919 and spanned 3,389 miles across twelve states. The age of the modern highway had begun!

But Fisher wasn't done. He then built the first North–South highway, the Dixie Highway. Cool.

Carl G. Fisher also did a lot of other interesting things.
(Look below the flying car for details.)

HEADLIGHT MILLIONAIRE

In 1904, Fisher—who had poor vision all his life—teamed up with an inventor to manufacture the first great headlights for cars. The venture was a success, and Fisher struck it rich.

FLYING CAR DEALER

In 1902, to demonstrate the sturdiness of the cars he was selling, Fisher pushed one off the roof of a tall building in Indianapolis. It was unharmed, and Fisher drove it away. Later, Fisher rigged a car to a hot-air balloon, climbed into the driver's seat, and drifted through the skies of Indianapolis. He loved to tell people he was the first person ever to fly a car across the city.

INDIANAPOLIS 500 FOUNDER

Wanting a place to test-drive his cars, Fisher co-built the Indianapolis Motor Speedway in 1909. And then in 1911, he founded America's most popular car race, the Indianapolis 500.

4

Perhaps Morgan's greatest invention, the traffic signal is everywhere. Just look below to see how many signals it takes to keep a small area of streets in order. And imagine what the world would be like without them! Collisions at every corner; timid drivers stuck at intersections for hours on end; little old ladies doing cartwheels over cars to cross the street. It's an ugly scene.

After witnessing a car accident, Garrett Morgan decided to act. Shortly after World War I, he introduced and patented a three-way traffic signal. Now, that's not to say that he necessarily invented the first traffic signal (that's a whole separate debate), but we believe in Garrett's invention. General Electric did, too. They bought the rights from him for $40,000.

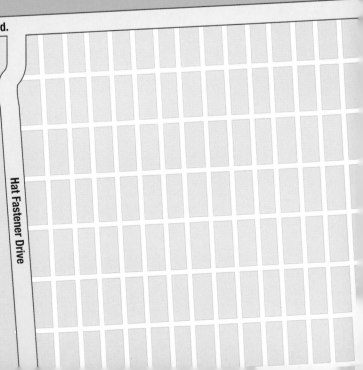

Three-Way Traffic Signal Memorial Expressway

Friction Drive Clutch Ave.

Safety Hood Highway

Cleveland Call Dr.

G. A. Morgan
Memorial Park

3

Hair Gel Blvd.

In the early 1900s, Garrett Morgan was running a successful business repairing sewing machines. A natural entrepreneur, he decided to tackle one of the industry's big problems. Sewing needles were working so fast that they were heating up and scorching the garments. Morgan began trying different chemicals that he thought might keep the needle from getting too hot.

One of the batches caused the hairs on the pony-fur cloth he was experimenting with to stand up. Morgan thought this was pretty neat, and tried the stuff out on his neighbor's dog. Same results. Morgan had accidentally invented the first "hair refining cream," paving the way for mohawks the world over.

Hat Fastener Drive

GARRETT AUGUSTUS MORGAN

1

Three-Way Traffic Signal Memorial Expressway

Overheating Sewing Needles St.

Our man Garrett here was born on March 4, 1877, in Paris, Kentucky, and was pretty busy for the rest of his life. He left home at fourteen with an elementary-school education under his belt, and made his way to Cleveland. There, he eventually married a gal named Mary Anne Hassek and had three sons. In addition to inventing the various products described on this page (pay attention to the street names, too!) Morgan did a great deal for the wellbeing of his fellow African Americans. He founded the *Cleveland Call* in 1920, a newspaper devoted to world news pertaining to black people. Finally, in 1963, he died a very tired man.

Cleveland Call Dr.

Garrett A. Morgan Pkwy.

Hair Gel Blvd.

2

Friction Drive Clutch Ave.

Carnegie Medal Rd.

In 1912, Morgan invented what he called a "safety hood." The safety hood was the precursor to the modern-day gas mask. As creepy as the gas mask looks, its intentions are good. Patented in 1914, Morgan's safety hood had an intake for fresh air and an exhaust for exhaled air.

The invention won acclaim from various safety organizations over the next few years, and in 1916, Morgan's safety hood had its greatest triumph. On July 24, an explosion trapped a number of workers in a tunnel under Lake Erie. The tunnel was filled with dangerous fumes and the rescue workers were unable to climb to safety. Morgan used the safety hood to climb into the tunnel and retrieve the workers, carrying them out on his back. The city of Cleveland bestowed Morgan with the Carnegie Medal and a Medal of Bravery. After the incident in the tunnel, safety hood orders began to come in from fire and police departments, as well as mining companies. In World War I, soldiers used Morgan's safety hood to protect themselves in battle from dangerous chlorine gas.

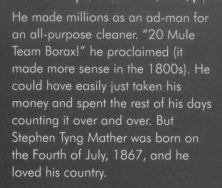

THE STORY

He made millions as an ad-man for an all-purpose cleaner. "20 Mule Team Borax!" he proclaimed (it made more sense in the 1800s). He could have easily just taken his money and spent the rest of his days counting it over and over. But Stephen Tyng Mather was born on the Fourth of July, 1867, and he loved his country.

Mather was an avid outdoorsman. His travels to various U.S. parks as a hiker and a mountaineer caused him great concern. In Yosemite, for example, there was a proposal to dam Hetch Hetchy Valley, and log and mine other parts.

His frustration with the state of the country's parks led him to appeal directly to the U.S. Secretary of the Interior, Franklin Lane. Lane invited him to come to Washington, D.C. to see if he couldn't do something about the problem himself. And so Mather went.

In order to protect parks, Mather knew he had to get the public and Congress to pay more attention to them. With his own money, Mather organized outdoor trips, inviting members of Congress and journalists to come see the lesser-explored corners of their homeland. Cooks came along to provide the intrepid explorers with venison and gravy, hot rolls, fresh pie, and fried chicken. Finally, in 1916, Congress created the National Park System and put Stephen Mather at its helm. From 1916 until 1929, Mather worked tirelessly to preserve parks and open them to the public. Mather suffered a stroke in 1928 and died in 1930. But to this day, parks around the country honor Mather's contribution in various ways. Why not get out there and find them?

92

STEPHEN MATHER

DEATH VALLEY

DENALI

GRAND CANYON

REDWOOD

ACADIA

SHENANDOAH

NATIONAL

CARLSBAD CAVERNS

MESA VERDE

AND THE

YELLOWSTONE

ARCHES

BIG BEND

CUYAHOGA VALLEY

GRAND TETON

HOTSPRINGS

HAWAII VOLCANOES

PARKS

EVERGLADES

YOSEMITE

93

CHER AMI*

A FEATHERED FRIEND
A FLYING HERO

* So here's the thing: Cher Ami was actually a French pigeon, but the Americans employed him during World War I. Still an American hero, we say.

During World War I, the U.S. Army employed over six hundred "carrier pigeons" to bring messages to different battle areas. One such pigeon was a bird by the name of Cher Ami. The name means "dear friend" in French, and Cher Ami proved to be a dear friend indeed.

Our hero successfully delivered twelve messages for the Americans. On his last flight in 1918, Cher Ami was hit by enemy fire, but nevertheless managed to complete his mission. Wounded in his chest and having lost a leg, he kept the message intact. The message was from the members of the 77th Infantry Division, who had been pinned down and separated from their allies. With the help of Cher Ami's message, 194 men in the battalion were located and rescued.

Cher Ami died from his battle wounds, but for his valor he was awarded several medals. His body was preserved and has been displayed at various museums around the U.S.

Hey look! It's (a model of) Cher Ami

BY THE WAY: *This little contraption on Cher Ami's neck is his message box.*

(1) FORREST CLARE ALLEN and his brothers grew up as athletic Missouri youngsters. Basketball was a relatively new sport, but the Allen brothers excelled at it. Forrest, in particular, was so good that in 1804, James Naismith, the founder of basketball, took notice and encouraged young Forrest to enroll at the University of Kansas where Naismith was the physical education director.

"PHOG"

(2) Allen accepted Naismith's invitation and joined up. Then, in 1906, Baker University in Kansas offered Allen a position coaching their basketball team. Naismith was skeptical and said, "You can't coach a game like basketball, Forrest. You play it."

HE'S THE MAN WHO

(3) Allen disagreed. He took the job at Baker and coached there from 1906 to 1908. He then returned to the University of Kansas to coach from 1908 to 1909. By the end of 1909, his teams had won 115 games and lost only 23. He decided it was as good a time as any to take a break from coaching.

(4) An interest in treating athletic injuries led Allen to enroll at the Central College of Osteopathy (bone and muscle medicine) in Kansas City. He graduated as a doctor and started practicing medicine. He coached here and there (his players started calling him "Doc") and even umpired some baseball games. His booming, foghorn-like voice earned him the nickname that we have come to know him by: PHOG.

(8) Why is Phog Allen important? He took something disorganized and unruly (old-school basketball) and turned it into the sport we all know today. He is known as the FATHER OF BASKETBALL COACHING, and finished his career with 744 wins and only 263 losses! Wow!

ALLEN

INVENTED MAN-TO-MAN

(7) Phog and an assistant coach developed the man-to-man defensive strategy, revolutionizing the game of basketball. Apparently people would just swarm the ball before Phog came up with this idea. Phog's team won another national championship in 1952, and he retired in 1956.

(5) Phog returned to the University of Kansas in 1920, where he would remain for many years. He led the team to back-to-back national championships in 1922 and 1923. In 1924, with the help of his wife, Phog finished his first book on basketball coaching and treating sports injuries, *My Basket-Ball Bible*.

(6) Phog was a vocal and effective spokesman for the sport of basketball. In 1936, Phog led the effort to make basketball an Olympic sport. In 1944, he exposed gambling as a serious problem in the sport. Players and referees were working together with gamblers to affect the outcome of games and make money.

BEULAH LOUISE HENRY
"THE LADY EDISON"*

Born in Memphis, Tennessee in 1887, Beulah Louise Henry was an inventor of the highest order. Throughout a long career creating toys and tools, she secured 49 patents, and was responsible for numerous other inventions.

Beulah attended Queens College and Elizabeth College in Charlotte, North Carolina. By the time she left Charlotte, she had already secured her first three patents. One was for a vacuum ice cream freezer, which helped cool ice cream quickly without the aid of too much ice (this was a big deal!). She also patented a handbag and an umbrella with removable colorful cloth sections intended to allow users to customize the look of their accessories.

In the 1920s, Beulah took her successful inventions to New York, where she started the Henry Umbrella and Parasol Company, and then later, the B.L. Henry Company of New York. She continued to work on inventions of various uses. She invented dolls that could move their eyes, their limbs, and their mouths. She came up with a sponge that came pre-loaded with soap in the middle. She invented a "protograph," which was basically an early version of a photocopier, allowing someone to get four copies out of a single sitting at a typewriter.

She worked with sewing machines and envelopes, and the widespread popularity of her devices landed her jobs with companies looking to utilize her unique creativity. She worked tirelessly for decades to introduce useful and delightful innovations. And for that, she was rewarded with public recognition and financial success. This set her apart from other female inventors of her generation.

Beulah became well-known throughout New York. Before her death in 1973, she developed a reputation as a writer, painter, and philanthropist, in addition to one of the great inventors of her time. Check out the facing page for some of the patents that Beulah obtained. While many of her inventions are no longer in use, if you think hard, you'll see her influence on all sorts of things we use today!

✳ This isn't a nickname we created for Beulah. "Lady Edison" is a name that people came up with for her in the 1930s. Really, Beulah was such an amazing inventor, she shouldn't be "Lady" anything. Beulah Henry was just herself. If anything, maybe we should call Edison "Gentleman Henry!"

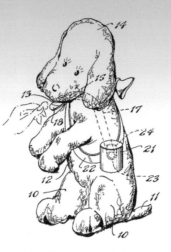

EATING TOY ANIMAL
Patent No. 2631408

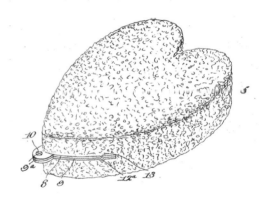

DOUBLE CHAIN STITCH
SEWING MACHINE
Patent No. 2037901

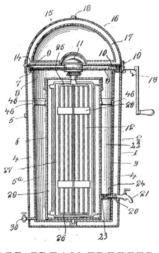

ICE CREAM FREEZER
Patent No. 1037762

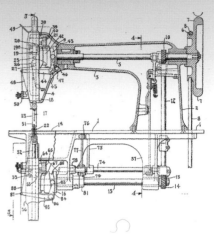

SOAP HOLDER
Patent No. 1577861

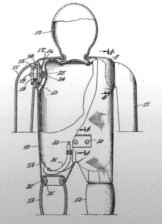

INFLATABLE DOLL
Patent No. 2503948

PARASOL
Patent No. 1492725

IT'S A "FROZEN

LITTLE FRANK EPPERSON was always something of a mad scientist. As a youngster in San Francisco, he would often dabble with mixing various flavors into soda water to create new drinks.

Then, one particularly cold night in 1905, he made a mistake. He left a cup of soda with a stirring stick in it out on the porch. The next morning Frank woke up, and when he walked outside, he found something remarkable.

The liquid had frozen. The stick was still lodged in the frozen soda. Seems simple enough, right? But up until then, no one had bothered to do this, and thus the popsicle was born.

Well, not quite.

Frank called his creation an "epsicle," a combination of his last name and the word "icicle," which he thought his product resembled. He shared his invention with family members and friends, but it wasn't until 17 years later that Frank realized he could sell his product. After presenting the epsicle at a firemen's ball, Frank had a hit. He started selling the frozen delight at amusement parks and other concessions stands around California, where masses of hot, thirsty, sweet-craving beach bums couldn't get enough of Frank's invention.

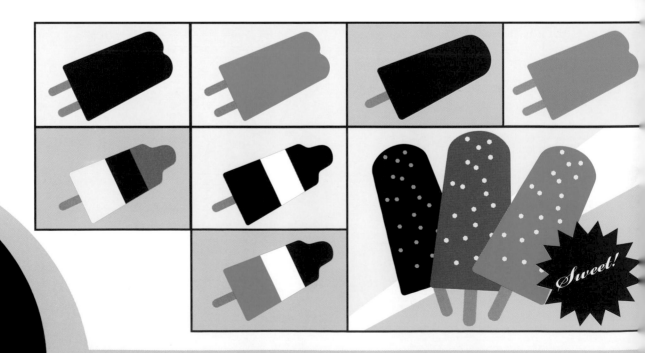

Sweet!

DRINK ON A STICK"!

Yay!

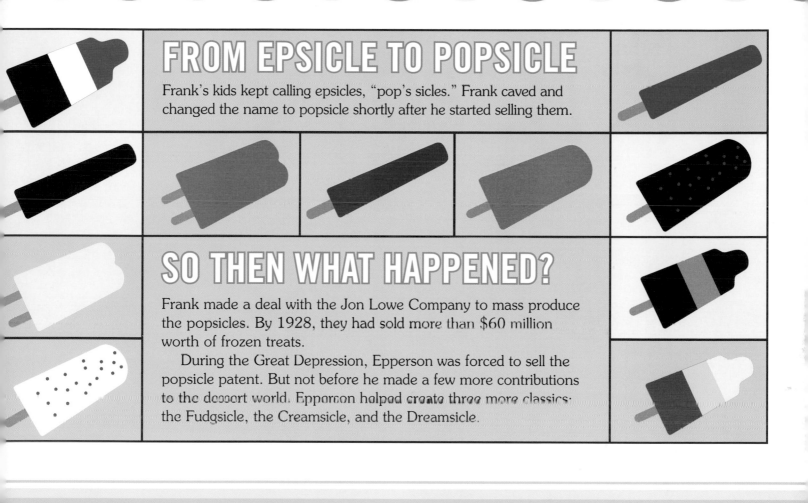

FROM EPSICLE TO POPSICLE

Frank's kids kept calling epsicles, "pop's sicles." Frank caved and changed the name to popsicle shortly after he started selling them.

SO THEN WHAT HAPPENED?

Frank made a deal with the Jon Lowe Company to mass produce the popsicles. By 1928, they had sold more than $60 million worth of frozen treats.

During the Great Depression, Epperson was forced to sell the popsicle patent. But not before he made a few more contributions to the dessert world. Epperson helped create three more classics: the Fudgsicle, the Creamsicle, and the Dreamsicle.

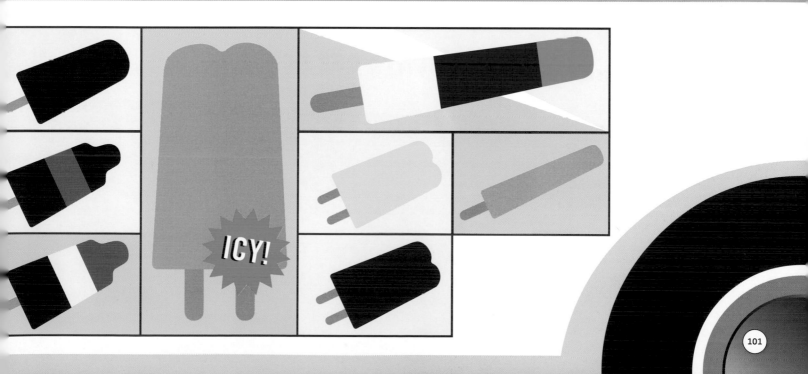

ICY!

RICHARD

DREW

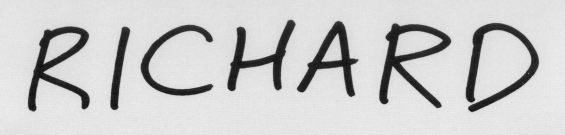

HIS THRIFTY ~~COOL~~ ADHESIVE TAPES HELPED OUR COUNTRY HOLD IT TOGETHER DURING THE GREAT DEPRESSION

Hi—this is the book pretending to speak in the voice of **Art Fry, co-inventor of Post-it notes.** Funny story: I (Art Fry) came up with Post-its in 1974, and they were first sold in '77, but they didn't really catch on until '80. (Sometimes, when you have a good idea, you gotta give it time to stick! But I digress.)

I'm not here to talk about my own personal adventures in adhesive innovation. **I'm here to talk about Richard Drew, the hardworking genius who invented adhesive tape.** Drew was hired by our company, 3M, back in 1921, when sandpaper was the biggest thing they had going.

Drew's breakthrough came in 1925: a masking–tape adhesive that could be stuck on a surface—and then removed—without damaging the surface! **(It may sound like nothing, but back then, it was something!)** And then, in 1928, he developed the world's first transparent tape, which led to over 900 more kinds of tape.

Now I know you're reading this book for fresh hero stories, so I'll share one more thing: **Tape arrived just in time for the Great Depression.** During that dark time, torn and broken items from clothing to lampshades to books were easily mended with tape. Tape made life just a little easier. That's real heroism.

Every kind of sticky tape you can think of— including all the tape surrounding me here—all owes a debt to Richard Drew's creative brain.

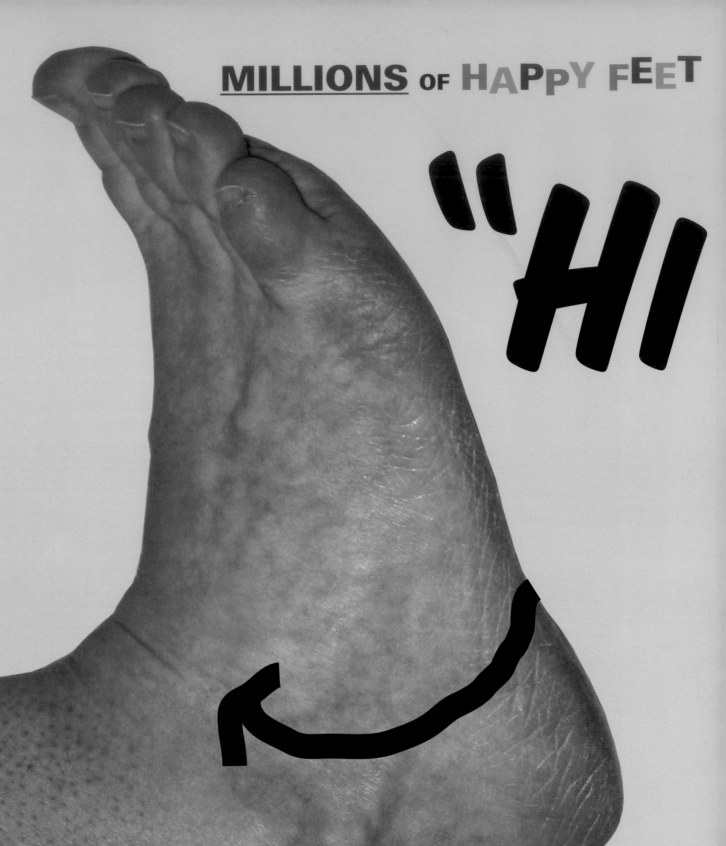

MILLIONS OF HAPPY FEET

"HI

This happy, healthy, actual-size (more or less) adult American foot has encountered Charles Brannock's quietly mighty 1926 invention—The Brannock Device™—more than 23 times! And more than 23 times, the foot has found a shoe that fits!*

* Please don't underestimate the value of a shoe that fits. Ill-fitting shoes lead to deadly foot diseases—really!

EVERYWHERE ARE STILL SAYING . . .

"GH FIVE" MR. BRANNOCK!! :)

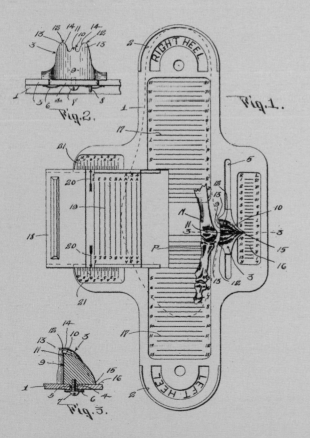

The Brannock Device— It Just Makes Feet Happier

As a college student in the 1920s, Charles F. Brannock of Syracuse, New York, monkeyed around with ideas for a better foot-measuring device.*

In 1926, Brannock built a prototype and put it to the test at his father's shoe store. The result? Unqualified success! The Brannock Device was born.

When the U.S. Navy began using the tool in the early 1930s, countless sailors' chronic foot problems were cured instantly. Their feet were fine, it turned out—they'd just been wearing the wrong-size shoes! By World War II, the whole military was using the Brannock Device, saving lots of people lots of pain.

Today, all these decades later, the Brannock Device—which Brannock manufactured in Syracuse until his death in 1992—remains the gold-standard tool for measuring the human foot.

BRANNOCK DEVICE (above)
I know you've had your feet measured by one of these things. If you say, "No I haven't," I won't believe you. Anyway, what are you waiting for? Go get measured! *Right now please.* (Didn't you read that note to the left???)

* Sure, the good ole wooden "RITZ stick" could give you an idea of the *LENGTH* of your foot. But Brannock knew the world was in sore need— literally!—of a tool that could easily measure the *WIDTH* and the *ARC* of a foot in addition to length. And that's just what he invented!

EVER NOTICE HOW CLEAN THE WASHINGTON MONUMENT LOOKS?

(OH, DIDN'T GET THAT WAY BY ITSELF.)

The National Memorials. They stand in memory of our nation's heroes. (That's why they're called *memorials*.)

Our memorials are built to last, but they're also fragile! Somebody's gotta take care of them. Without careful preservation, the National Memorials would fall apart, and then we'd probably forget everything. So here's my point: Let's take a moment to recognize the people who keep our National Memorials in great shape, so that future U.S. citizens can keep on remembering our country's great *non*-forgotten heroes.

BUT FIRST, TO GET YOU INTO THE CELEBRATING MOOD, HERE ARE SOME IMPRESSIVE FACTS ABOUT THE WASHINGTON MONUMENT.....

STEEP STRUCTURE, STEEP CLEANING BILL, STEEP RESPECT FOR OUR NATION'S PRICELESS HERITAGE.

The monument was cleaned and restored between 1997 and 2001, at a cost of over 9 million dollars. (The scaffolding alone was about 3 million.) At the National Park Service's behest, the scaffolding was specially designed so that it only surrounded (and did not touch) the surface of the monument, in order to prevent any possible damage.

OLD, YES. OBSOLETE? NEVER.

The Washington Monument is the oldest National Memorial. Construction started in 1848, but money was so tight, it took 36 years to finish. The least we can do is take care of the thing.

A LOT OF SWAYING STONE TO KEEP FROM FALLING ON PEOPLE'S HEADS.

The Washington Monument is over 555 feet (170 m) high, making it the world's tallest stone structure. When it's really windy out, the monument sways just a little bit. (Good thing the structure is checked and restored from time to time.)

THANK YOU

EAR CLEANERS OF THE
LINCOLN MEMORIAL

GREAT JOB

NOSE REPAIRERS OF
MOUNT RUSHMORE

NICE WORK

UNDERAPPRECIATED MAINTAINERS
OF THE AWESOME TRAM SYSTEM
INSIDE THE ST. LOUIS GATEWAY ARCH

WHY NOT MAIL A THANK-YOU NOTE TO THE MEN &
WOMEN WHO PRESERVE YOUR NATIONAL MEMORIALS?

YOU CAN MAIL A THANK-YOU NOTE ANYTIME TO "ARCHITECTURAL CONSERVATOR, NATIONAL PARK SERVICE, 1100 OHIO DRIVE SW, WASHINGTON, DC 20242"

(BY THE WAY: IF YOU ACTUALLY DO THIS, THEY'LL BE COMPLETELY BLOWN AWAY. THESE PEOPLE DON'T GET TOO MANY THANK-YOU NOTES.)

Floretta Doty McCutcheon

America's Queen of BOWLING

	1	2	3	4	5	6	7	8	9	10	Total
Flo	✗	✗	✗	✗	✗	✗	/	/	✗	✗	/

Floretta McCutcheon excelled in a sport dominated by men. She was a bowler, and a fine one at that. Having never bowled until she was well over thirty, she stared down the odds and defied what people expected from people of her gender and her age.

As there were few female bowlers in Floretta's time, she mainly competed against men. Shortly before **McCutcheon** turned forty, she bested the world champion **Jimmy Smith** in a three-game exhibition match, securing her place as the best female bowler of the 1930s. Throughout her career, she bowled ten perfect games (knocking down every pin in every frame). Floretta kept bowling into her seventies, and paved the way for a generation of female bowlers after her.

While girls these days might not be fighting to get a lane at the local alley, Floretta's accomplishments paved the way for young girls to play the sports that they love today. It took talented women like Floretta standing up and playing the same games as men for Americans to see that women are as resilient and athletic as their male counterparts. For more forgotten heroes of women's sports, check out page 156.

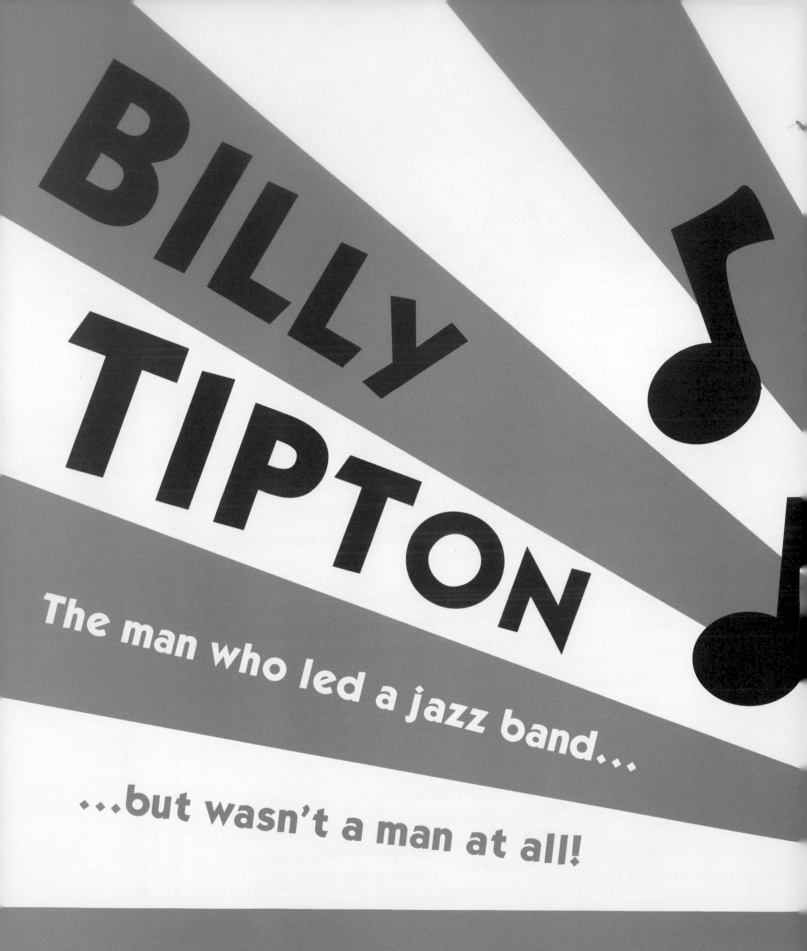

BILLY TIPTON

The man who led a jazz band...

...but wasn't a man at all!

IN 1989
a jazz musician by the name of
Billy Tipton died of an ulcer. Upon his death,
paramedics discovered something quite unusual. Billy was
not a man at all. Billy Tipton was actually Dorothy Tipton, and she
had been living disguised as a man for more than fifty years!
Dorothy first adopted her male persona as a young musician trying to
make her way in the 1930s. She could play the violin, organ, saxophone, and piano
with the best of them, but it was difficult for female musicians to make it in the jazz
scene. So Dorothy disguised herself as Billy, and from the 1930s to the 1970s, she lived
and performed as him. Even her closest bandmates had no idea that Billy was not
a man. She played for a decade with two other men in the Billy Tipton Trio, and neither
of them ever had any suspicions about Billy's true gender.
Billy Tipton was known across the country for her musical prowess. Yet nobody knew that
she was a woman succeeding in a role traditionally reserved for men. People assumed that
women couldn't be as skilled as male musicians, but Billy proved everyone wrong with
her talent. Although we remember her now for the illusion she managed to pull off,
the fact is Billy only adopted her male disguise because she felt she had to. She
lived her life as a man, because she believed that people wouldn't give her
a chance as a woman performer. But now that the world knows who
Billy Tipton was, let's salute her for who she really was: a
great jazz musician.

THREE CHEERS FOR LABOR UNIONS!

In the 19th and early 20th centuries, people worked twelve hours a day, six days a week. Kids, too. Forget about soccer practice and Saturday morning cartoons. School? Yeah right. Fun? Only if you're not too exhausted and broken down by work.

Beginning in the 18th century, workers started joining together to form labor unions. The idea was that if everyone pulled their demands together, their bosses couldn't continue to overwork them or underpay them. The Industrial Revolution had created a whole slew of unsafe factory jobs that worked men, women, and children to the bone for very little money.

Still, for years, employers fought labor unions and legislators who wanted to shorten the work week, and create safer working conditions. And, for the most part, they were successful.

Then, in the 1930s, workers and unions had their real heyday. The Great Depression was taking its toll on already-mistreated workers, and lawmakers were sympathetic. In 1934, years of efforts by labor unions paid off. Congress passed the Fair Labor Standards Act, which set a minimum wage (25 cents/hour), and a maximum workweek of 44 hours. People who worked more than 44 hours would get extra overtime pay.

The five-day workweek was finally a reality!

Oh, and one more little thing. No more child labor! Kids under fourteen could no longer legally work. There were still some loopholes that allowed for agricultural jobs and family businesses, but overall children wouldn't have to be skulking around in dark mine shafts, or be cooped up in windowless factories sewing clothes. Hello Saturdays!

DECEMBER 1915

"Wake me up when someone invents the weekend."

MONDAY	TUESDAY	WEDNESDAY	THURSDAY	FRIDAY	SATURDAY	SUNDAY
		1	2	3 WORK	4	5
6 WORK	7 WORK	8 WORK	9 WORK	10 WORK	11 WORK!	12 WORK
13 W	14 O	15 ↓	16 ↘	17 WORK WORK WORK	18 ~~DAY OFF!~~ WORK...	19 ~~DAY OFF?~~ WORK
20 WORK	21	22	23 WORK	24 WORKMAS EVE	25 CHRISTMAS/ WORK 🎄	26 WORK
27	28	29 WORK	30	31		

(SPAM)

WHAT DOES A HERO LOOK LIKE?

WELL, IT'S RECTANGULAR.

AND KIND OF FIRM.

IT'S PINKISH.

IT'S SORT OF COVERED IN JELLY.

IT LOOKS LIKE SPAM!

SPAM has gotten a bad rap. Why are people so down on it? Is it because of its pungent smell? Is it because of the unnatural shape? Is it because it's just so easy to make fun of a lump of meat that plops out of a can?

Well, believe it or not, SPAM isn't just a punchline (or a name for unwanted email). It's something that has helped a lot of people through tough times.

In 1937, with many Americans suffering the financial effects of the Great Depression, Jay Hormel presented a pork product that would last indefinitely (given the right conditions, SPAM can last forever in the can) and would feed people cheaply. SPAM—a mixture of pork, ham, sugar, salt, and a few other extras—was an instant success.

A few years later, with the beginning of World War II, SPAM had its real chance to shine. American and Russian soldiers alike kept from going hungry by turning to SPAM. Likewise, Americans back home, trying to conserve money and resources for the war effort, ate SPAM. And the people being liberated by the Allied Forces? They ate SPAM.

Today, the average American kid probably hasn't even tasted SPAM. But in certain pockets of the world like Hawaii and Korea, SPAM is still a huge hit. So next time, before you turn up your nose at a can of SPAM, remember that it just might have been the meat that won the war.

This is Babe Ruth.

I normally use a baseball bat to drive my point home, but this morning I woke up and decided to try something different.

I promised myself I'd wear this beard until you fully understand the greatness that was Josh Gibson. A great catcher, a world-class hitter—that was Gibson. The man could flat *play ball*.

The trouble is, you weren't there to see Gibson swing. You weren't there for the home runs—you didn't witness the thrills.

How, then, can I expect you to really understand the man? The truth is, you can't. Not fully, anyway.

I guess I'll be wearing this false beard for the rest of the day.

DISCLAIMER — The editors of this book cannot verify whether the great Babe Ruth actually held Josh Gibson in high esteem. In fact, if Gibson was indeed as great a hitter as Ruth (and there's no way to fairly compare them, because Josh Gibson wasn't allowed to swing at baseballs thrown by white men), Ruth might have been extremely jealous of Gibson. Now, I don't know how much you've read about Babe Ruth, but if you've read half as much as I have, you're going to agree that there's a better-than-good chance that a jealous Babe Ruth would be a tad less magnanimous when speaking about Josh Gibson than we've imagined him here.

JOSH GIBSON

Known as the "Black Babe Ruth" for his home-run prowess, Josh Gibson played catcher for the Pittsburgh Crawfords and the Homestead Grays in baseball's Negro Leagues from 1930 to 1946.

Because he was black, Gibson never had the opportunity to play in the Major Leagues. In January 1947—just three months before Jackie Robinson debuted with the Brooklyn Dodgers as the first black player in Major League Baseball history—Gibson died of a stroke. He was 36 years old.

In 1935, Babe Ruth retired with 714 homers, a Major League record that stood for almost 40 years. But according to a small plaque in the Baseball Hall of Fame, Josh Gibson retired with "almost 800." (The number is not technically official, but it's not bad!)

ALMOST 800 CAREER HOME RUNS

Satchel Paige, who was once Gibson's teammate and also the first black Major Leaguer to be elected to the Hall of Fame, called Gibson "the greatest hitter who ever lived."

PHILIP JOHNSON
AND THE
NAVAJO
CODE TALKERS

The Code Talker Alphabet

A: Woh-la-chee (Ant)
B: Na-hash-chid (Badger)
C: Moasi (Cat)
D: Be (Deer)
E: Dzeh (Elk)
F: Ma-e (Fox)
G: Klizzie (Goat)
H: Lin (Horse)
I: Tkin (Ice)
J: Tkele-cho-gi (Jackass)
K: Klizzie-yazzie (Kid)

L: Dibeh-Yazzie (Lamb)
M: Na-as-tsosi (Mouse)
N: Nesh-chee (Nut)
O: Ne-ahs-jah (Owl)
P: Bi-sodih (Pig)
Q: Ca-yeilt (Quiver)
R: Gah (Rabbit)
S: Dibeh (Sheep)
T: Than-zie (Turkey)
U: No-da-ih (Ute)
V: A-keh-di-glini (Victor)
W: Gloe-ih (Weasel)
X: Al-a-as-dzoh (Cross)

Y: Tsah-az-zih (Yucca)
Z: Besh-do-gliz (Zinc)

A Few Specialized Terms

Major General: So-na-kih
   (Two Stars)
Colonel: Astah-besh-legai
   (Silver Eagle)
Fighter plane: Da-he-tih-hi
   (Hummingbird)
Destroyer: Ca-lo (Shark)
Transport Plane: Astah (Eagle)

THE NAVAJO CODE TALKERS

For American soldiers fighting Japan in World War II, secure communications were of the utmost importance. However, Japanese intelligence officers were so good at deciphering codes that the Americans had to change theirs every 24 hours. That is, until a World War I veteran named Philip Johnson suggested employing Native American Navajos. Johnson had spent a great deal of time with Navajo people in his youth and had come to admire their customs and traditions, as well as their oral language (there is no written version. The key on the previous page shows phonetic pronunciations). Navajo proved to be an ideal language to use as a code. There were believed to be only thirty non-Navajos in the world who could speak it.

In 1942, twenty-nine Navajos joined the Marines. This group of "code talkers" developed a means of communicating secretly, by assigning each letter of the alphabet an English word that started with that letter (like, ant for a, badger for b, etc.). The Navajos would then translate those English words to Navajo. For example, say a code talker wanted to communicate the letter "A" to another soldier. He would say the word *woh-la-chee*. The code talker on the other end would translate that to the English word "ant," and recognize that ant begins with "A," the letter being sent. Make sense? Well, the Japanese couldn't figure it out. Supposedly, even other Navajos who didn't know the code found it impossible to decipher. Few people spoke Navajo, and even fewer could speak both Navajo and English. The code was never broken.

By 1943, 400 Navajo Code Talkers were in service. They took part in every battle in the Pacific between 1942 and 1945, often risking their lives in extremely dangerous situations in order to get information to other soldiers.

The Navajo code was so valuable that the U.S. government kept it a secret until 1968, in case they ever needed it again!

your broken mosttalented hocolate lion pants forever!

passports 4 tiny country

vel to France $80 in the compartment cial airplane. not cramped ted like a pet a squirrel 1-555-1322.

SQUEEZERS r old oranges an carrot tops ancy furniture. one by hand rotten fruit. nly standard add poodles eezerbros.net

ride to the se races, n Embassy, ck market, ple taxicab ur needs DOGSLEDS very slowly!

- We'll find it! emote control? your keys or e even love! 555-LOST.

tally us! that bad.

Services Directory
Find the right person for the job!

SERVICES

AXE SHARPENING

Axe-llent Sharpening -- We'll sharpen, hone, and polish yr blades for less $$. Chop down trees with the bst of them!

★ ★ HATCHET HANDLERS ★ ★
Dull blades? Call us and we will try to make them less dull. 555-5421

BEAR TRAINING *THANKS*

BERNIE'S BEAR OBEDIENCE SCHOOL
Disobedient Bear? Our teachers are highly trained and ready to help. From unwanted burrowing, tree scratching, maulings, and garbage scrounging, to performance anxiety, we will diagnose and train your bear to behave better.

G U A R A N T E E D .

★ ★ ★ ★ ★ ★ ★ ★

We service more bear owners in the area than any other bear obedience school. Your bear will be nurtured in the friendly confines of our 3,000-acre facility, and share space with the 2,600 other urban bears we help. We've been servicing bear owners for almost 60 years. Space is extremely limited. Applicants must fill out our 2,000-page application for consideration of enrollment in Bernie's Bear School. Call 1-555-BAD-BEAR.

FINANCIAL SERVICES

MONEY STORAGE
$$$$$$$$$$$$$$
We have more than four mattresses for you to hide your hard-earned $$ under. Call us. Available in King, Qn, Dbl, Bnk.
HideYourMoneyUnderMyMattress.com

GARDENING

GREEN MEANIES
Local professionals will shape bushes into animals for you. We can do elphnts or jellyfish. Othr anmls coming soon. 555-1682

GENERAL SERVICES

FRED W. DEMARA
GENERAL SERVICEMAN
Why pay more for less? I'm trained in any number of trades. You name it, I'll help you out. Need a surgeon? I'm your man. College dean? Teacher? Look no further! 555-FRED.

STEVE
You break it, Steve fix it. No worries. 555-4123

NOTICE TO READERS REGARDING: *UH OH...*
FERDINAND WALDO DEMARA, JR.: GENERAL SERVICE PROVIDER

One of the greatest imposters in history, Ferdinand Demara, fooled countless people for almost 40 years. As a youngster, Demara was devastated when his father lost his job and his house in 1932. He would never really be the same. Demara first tried the religious life, entering a Trappist monastery to become a monk. Later, he would enter the Army, then the Navy. After deserting both, he used fake credentials to become a teacher, a philosophy student, and the dean of a college. He was then imprisoned for 18 months for deserting the Army, but when he emerged, he started up as an imposter again. Perhaps the most impressive of all his feats was when he joined the Canadian Navy as a surgeon, serving the crew during the Korean War with little more than a few books to help him. In fact, thanks to a sharp memory, he was able to perform all of his fake jobs with skill. Was he a villain, or just a man trying to prove himself to the world? Either way, be wary of hiring anyone who says they've been a: *HA*

- Trappist monk
- Law student
- Psychology PhD
- College dean
- Cancer researcher
- Zoologist
- Hospital orderly
- Soldier
- Sailor
- Assistant warden
- Deputy sheriff
- Schoolteacher
- Physician and medical officer with the Royal Canadian Navy
  AND a
- Hospital chaplain!

JOB LISTINGS

AARDVARK TAILOR

ANIMAL PANTS, INC. needs an experienced tailor to fit aardvarks for jeans, slacks, overalls, etc. 555-4325

ASSISTANT WARDEN

TEXAS DEPARTMENT OF CORRECTIONS

SEEKS TOUGH BUT FAIR ASSISTANT WARDEN FOR HUNTSVILLE PRISON

Have you ever been an inmate yourself? Maybe you were imprisoned briefly for deserting the military? Is your knowledge of the inner workings of a prison better for it? Well then you just might be the right person for the job! We're looking for a reform-minded assistant warden to treat prisoners humanely. We won't check your background, or ask many questions.

Call us at: 555-4201

DEAN OF PHILOSOPHY

GANNON COLLEGE
of Erie, Pennsylvania is looking for a Dean for the School of Philosophy.

DRY WELL WETTER

★ ★ ★ ★ DIRT TO MUD ★ ★ ★ ★
We need a few strong men to help us pour water into dry wells. $300K/yr. www.FantasyJobs.com/dirttomud.ha

FOOT MASSAGE TESTER

I love foot massages, but I hate bad foot massages. I will pay you to test out foot massages for me and let me know if they are good enough for me. Call Chester Featherstone, 555-4192.

SCHOOL TEACHER

TEACH STUDENTS LATIN AND FRENCH IN BEAUTIFUL NORTH HAVEN, MAINE

Come visit us at our campus.

ZOOLOGIST

Experienced zoologist needed. Graduate degree required. Credentials

not checked
by calling

FOR S

FAMILY FO

Actors wi
pretend to
family. Pe
impress y
bosses, g
even you

OLD FOOD

Leftover ho
salad, eggs
sandwiches,
orange juic

PURPLE S

Slight wear
so
po
a
di

JOHN STAPP

b. 1910   (M.D., Ph.D., and U.S. Air Force Colonel)   d. 1999

→ Death eventually got him down to Ø m.p.h.* and Ø g.n.i.p.h.,* but that's nothing to be ashamed of.

*miles per hour   #great new ideas per hour

HIS VISION FOR DUMMIES AND SEAT BELTS MADE US SAFER

In the 1950s, John Stapp said, "Hey guys, let's use Air Force crash dummies in car-crash safety tests."
The Air Force frowned — "We are not the Car Force," they moaned—but Stapp got 'em to fund the car tests anyway.*
The rest is history. After America saw dummies getting smashed up in car wrecks, it got convinced real fast that seat belts are good.

THIS GUY WAS ON FIRE WITH SMART CAR-SAFETY IDEAS NOBODY WANTED

1. **HAND-OPERATED POWER BRAKES.** (The hand is quicker than the foot, Stapp argued. Car companies sighed.)
2. **REAR-FACING PASSENGER SEATS.** (Rear-facing passengers are much safer, Stapp argued. Car companies rolled their eyes.)

*He convinced them, the story goes, by presenting the statistic that more Air Force pilots were dying in car crashes than in plane crashes.

(Do you see what made John Stapp special? Not only did he have great ideas, he had a special flair for communicating them. That flair made all the difference. Plus, he was brave.)

To study the effects of superfast acceleration and deceleration on the human body, Air Force Colonel John Stapp strapped himself to rocket sleds he designed and built with volunteer help. (Stapp, a medical doctor, repaid his volunteers with free family health care.)

Stapp's sleds jetted him to speeds of up to 632 mph (1,017 km/h)— faster than anyone on land had ever traveled. Then they stopped instantly, simulating a crash. (He once stopped so fast he went blind for a day — all his head's blood had flown into his eyes!)

Stapp's research led the way to safer airplane design and, eventually, safer car design. (Did you see those notes on the left page about Stapp and seat belts? This guy was a safety juggernaut.)

Use this word as much as possible, please.

I'M ALSO THE PERSON WHO COINED THE FAMOUS PHRASE **"MURPHY'S LAW"**

THE PHRASE GOES LIKE THIS:
"IF ANYTHING CAN GO WRONG, IT WILL GO WRONG."
THEREFORE, BE SAFE. BE SMART. BE THOROUGH. BEFORE YOU RIDE A ROCKET SLED, TEST IT. THEN RE-TEST IT. THEN RE-RE-TEST IT..... IF YOU MUST BE A DAREDEVIL, BE A CAUTIOUS ONE.

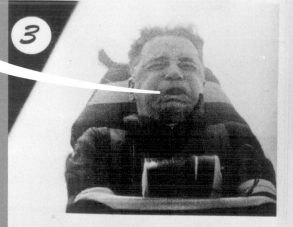
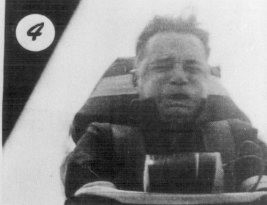

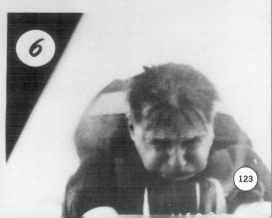

These six photos show John Stapp enduring extreme acceleration and deceleration in a rocket-powered research sled in 1954.

Pictures 1 thru 3 show Stapp in the first five seconds of acceleration, as the sled shot up to 421 mph (677 km/h). Pictures 4 thru 6 show the effect of sudden, crash-like deceleration.

One of Stapp's goals in testing the sleds on himself (instead of, say, a chimpanzee) was to develop a first-hand understanding of what extreme acceleration and deceleration felt like.

(It made him feel like barfing.)

* Before Edwin Land invented the instant camera, a few cameras called themselves "instant," but these were just film-development labs in miniature. Land's Polaroid camera was an all-new technology: push a button, wait sixty seconds, and voila—a picture! True instant photography.

IN 1943…

Edwin Land's three-year old daughter asked a question about taking photos: "Why can't I see the pictures <u>now</u>?"

→

DID LAND RESPOND…

"Sweetie, instant photography is impossible. You just need to be patient and wait, like everyone else, for the film to get processed"?

→

NO WAY!

Instead, Land invented self-developing film, and a camera to go with it: the Polaroid Model 95, launched in 1948.

→

PEOPLE LOVED 'EM!

Polaroid sold tens of millions of instant-film cameras in sixty years, before the technology was put to rest in 2008. Although digital cameras have taken over, some people still prefer instant film.

→

1972 MODEL
(first to take pictures this classic size and shape)

COPS STILL LOVE 'EM!

Easy to shoot and almost impossible to manipulate, instant photos remain tiny unsung heroes in some police detectives' everyday work.

→

DR. EDWIN LAND WAS NO DOCTOR.

He was just a self-taught scientific genius who got called "doctor" a lot. (He tried Harvard twice, but never graduated.)

→

HIS SUIT SOMETIMES GOT VERY SMELLY.

When Land got going on a train of thought, he didn't stop the train. He once wore a suit for eighteen straight days.

→

IN 1982…

Edwin Land retired with 533 patents, all of them related to his films and cameras. His refinement of instant photography had been a tireless, lifelong pursuit.

→

"My **whole life** has been spent trying to teach people that **intense concentration** for hour after hour can bring out **resources** you didn't know you had."

(ACTUAL QUOTE)

ALBERT I

THE HISTORY OF AMERICAN ANIMAL ASTRONAUTS IS FILLED WITH

COURAGEOUS BEASTS OF ALL SORTS, FROM BACTERIA AND INSECTS, TO MICE

AND DOGS. IN 1948, A RHESUS MONKEY NAMED ALBERT II FAMOUSLY BECAME

THE FIRST OF HIS KIND TO BE SUCCESSFULLY LAUNCHED INTO THE FINAL

FRONTIER, EARNING HIMSELF A PLACE IN OUR NATIONAL HISTORY.

BUT WHAT ABOUT HIS NAMESAKE? LET'S NOT FORGET THE ORIGINAL ALBERT!

ALBERT I, BLESS HIS SOUL, IS THE FORGOTTEN HERO OF ANIMAL SPACE

TRAVEL. HAD HE NOT BEEN THE FIRST MONKEY TO GIVE HIS LIFE TO THE SPACE

PROGRAM...WELL, ANOTHER MONKEY PROBABLY WOULD HAVE. BUT STILL,

WHEN ALBERT I CLIMBED ABOARD A V-2 ROCKET ON JUNE 11, 1948, HE

VENTURED WHERE MAN HAD YET TO GO. A MERE 9 LBS (4 KG), TINY ALBERT

WAS THE ROCKET'S ONLY CARGO. SADLY, ALBERT DID NOT SURVIVE LONG

ENOUGH TO BE THE FIRST MONKEY IN SPACE, BUT HE REMAINS AN INTREPID

SIMIAN AND INDEED WORTHY OF PRAISE, SO LET'S TAKE A MOMENT TO

CELEBRATE THE LIFE OF OUR DEAR DEPARTED MONKEY FRIEND!

BROWNIE WISE

The Single Mom who Saved Tupperware, Inspired a Thousand Businesswomen, Made Her Boss Jealous, ...and Lost Her Job!

BROWNIE WISE, who blazed a new trail for businesswomen during the 1940s and '50s, always dreamed big.

AS A YOUNG WIFE in the '30s, Brownie Wise wrote for the *Detroit News*, spinning fanciful yarns about a made-up childhood on a made-up Southern plantation. She'd also invent stories for the paper about her wonderful life at home. But in reality, her husband was abusive, and Wise divorced him in 1942.

TUPPERWARE PARTY, EARLY 1950s — Brownie Wise presents Tupperware products to a group of friends in her own living room. For fun, the guests wear impromptu hats fashioned from the plastic containers. Wise's parties, which combined shopping with socializing, helped America get comfortable with the idea of storing food in plastic containers. (At the time, these were new and even sort of intimidating.)

WITH A MOTHER AND BABY TO SUPPORT, Wise got to thinking about running her own business. Plastic Tupperware containers were brand new at the time, and hardly anybody got the point. Without someone to demonstrate the innovative "Tupper seal"—which made a weird *burp* sound to let you know the container was sealed air-tight—sales at stores were low. Brownie and her mother took matters into their own hands and started a business called Tupperware Patio Parties. They would invite people over and, while munching on cookies and making conversation, demonstrate and sell the burping containers. It was fun.

SO THEN EARL TUPPER, the brilliant but introverted head of Tupperware, got word of how many containers Brownie was selling and made the "wise" decision to hire her as the vice president of a new Tupperware Home Parties division. Soon, women around the country— hundreds, then thousands—were joining in and starting their own businesses selling Tupperware at parties. (By this point, Tupperware wasn't even sold in stores anymore.) Brownie Wise traveled all over the country, speaking at conferences and giving lectures on her successful model that put women at the center of business. In 1954, she became the first woman to ever appear on the cover of *Business Week* magazine.

AS WISE'S FAME GREW, Earl Tupper became jealous. People were saying that Wise was responsible for the success of Tupperware! In 1958, Tupper fired her. Wise didn't have any stock in the company, and was left with just one year's severance pay—a year's more than she was going to get until fellow executives stepped in. Wise didn't let it get her down, though. She went on to start up her own businesses selling cosmetics. To this day, companies like Mary Kay continue to draw on Brownie Wise's business formula for success.

BOTTs DOTS

- 1953 -
Dr. Elbert D. Botts is
working for the California
Department of Transportation. He's trying to
come up with a durable way to alert motorists
that they are drifting into other lanes. Painted lines
are okay, but they fade away, and sleepy drivers can't
tell when they've started veering over the lines. Botts's
solution? Simple. Raised pavement markers, a.k.a.
those bumps between lanes on the highway, a.k.a.
BOTTS DOTS. Haven't given much thought to them,
huh? Well these little road bumps are pretty
important. The next page illustrates just
how Botts Dots can save
your life!

1 YOU'RE DRIVING TO THE GROCERY STORE. THE SUMMER SUN IS WARMING THE CAR, AND YOU HAVE A GENERAL SENSE OF HAPPINESS AND SATISFACTION.

2 UH OH. THAT SATISFACTION AND HAPPINESS HAVE TURNED INTO SOMETHING MORE AKIN TO SLEEPINESS. YOU START DRIFTING OFF TO SLUMBERLAND.

3 ALL OF A SUDDEN YOUR CAR STARTS SHAKING. WHAT IN THE WORLD IS GOING ON?!? LOOKS LIKE YOU JUST GOT BOTTS DOTTED! YOUR CAR RAN OVER A LINE OF RAISED BUMPS THAT SEPARATES YOUR LANE FROM THE NEXT, JOLTING YOU BACK FROM YOUR BRIEF NAP.

4 WELL, YOU'RE DEFINITELY AWAKE NOW. YOU DRIVE ON, STARTLED, BUT GRATEFUL THAT YOUR SHORT BOUT OF SLEEPYTIME DIDN'T CAUSE YOU TO GET INTO AN ACCIDENT.

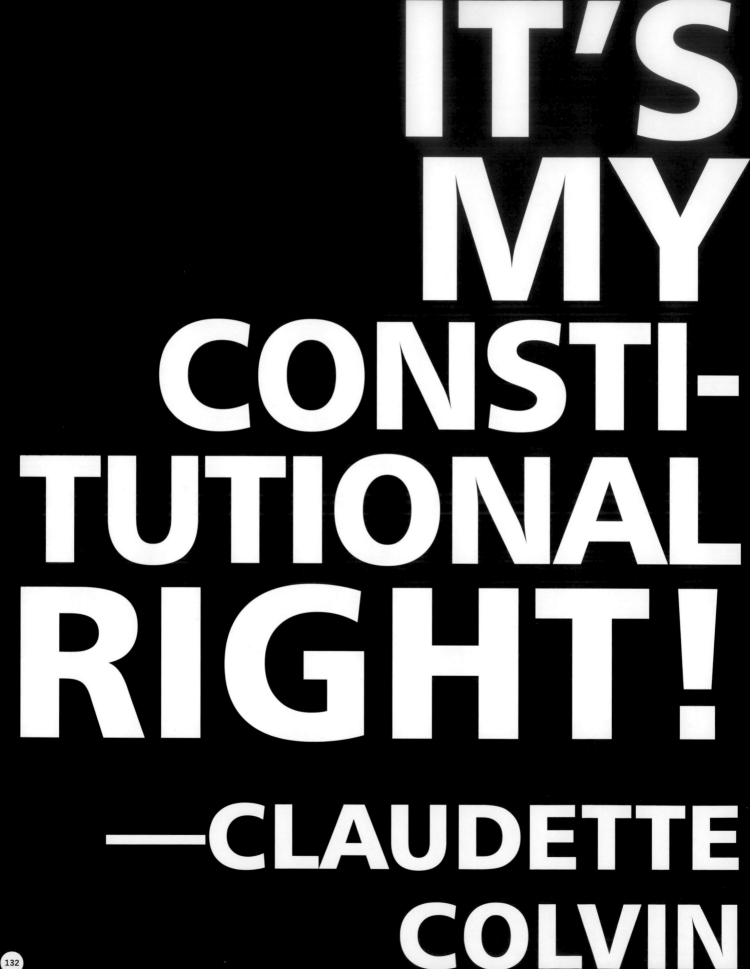

IT'S MY CONSTI- TUTIONAL RIGHT!

—CLAUDETTE COLVIN

15-YEAR-OLD

Claudette Colvin was just doing what she thought was right. Earlier that month, her teacher, Miss Nesbitt, had taught her about the Fourteenth Amendment. No State shall "deprive any person of life, liberty, or property, without due process of law; nor deny to any person within its jurisdiction the equal protection of the laws," Miss Nesbitt said. So why shouldn't Claudette get to sit wherever she wanted to sit on the bus?

It was March 2, 1955, and nine months later, an African-American woman named ROSA PARKS would become famous for refusing to give up her seat on a bus to white passengers.

But this was right now. Claudette had no idea who Rosa Parks was. She only knew that people were telling her that because she was black, she would have to give up her seat on the bus. SHE REFUSED.

The police showed up to arrest Colvin. They pulled young Claudette off the bus, handcuffed her, and placed her in the back of a squad car. As she was being dragged from the bus, she could be heard shouting, "It's my Constitutional right!" The civil rights community was outraged. They hired a lawyer by the name of Martin Luther King, Jr.—yup, *the* MARTIN LUTHER KING, JR.—to help defend Claudette in court. However, some leaders were unsure whether or not Claudette was the right person to spark a movement. Some believed she was too young. Others thought she was too immature or irresponsible to be a leader of her community.

For whatever reason, Claudette slowly faded out of sight. Rosa Parks would eventually become the face of the Montgomery Bus Boycott, which took the civil rights movement to a new level of urgency.

Nowadays, Claudette Colvin is a retired nursing-home nurse. Fifty years have passed since the day of her brave act. However, Claudette's influence should not be underestimated. While she never rose to national prominence, she got people's attention, and, at the tender age of fifteen, demonstrated what it truly means to stand up for what you believe in... by sitting down.

Have you ever used anything?

Have you ever used a book? No? Well how about a pen, a shirt, or a cup? No? Really? OK, how about a computer, or cinnamon handcuffs? You've surely used both a computer and cinnamon handcuffs.

Listen: If you've ever used anything at all—a phone, a wig, a gruydad, or a magnetized ham—then you have benefited from containerization.

What is containerization?

Well, after anything gets made—a fire ladder, a cotton ball, anything—it has to get from point A (wherever it got made) to point Z (your hands). Containerization makes this happen smoothly.

Before the 1950s, getting stuff from factories to people sometimes required many rounds of packing

58,140
rolls of toilet paper

12,383
pairs of shoes

1,584
saxophones

and unpacking. Moving cargo between ships, trains, planes, and trucks was an unbelievably time-consuming process, and it demanded an enormous amount of sweaty, thankless labor.

Containerization, a process developed in the 1950s by Malcom McLean and other smart shippers, made it so that almost everything in the world now gets transported in one kind of large, rectangular, metal container (pictured here).

Thanks to the underappreciated art of containerization, a shipment of 21,235 books can get packed in Singapore, boated to New York, trucked to New Jersey, flown to Tennessee, and moved by train to Texas—all without ever being unpacked, repacked, or even opened! If it sounds boring, it's not. It's amazing. It changed the world.

Containerization may not be your hero, personally, but it's the hero of everybody who uses things.

3,850
laptop computers

190,290
DVD movies

14,402
something-or-others

21,235
books

LEARNING KUNG FU
WITH
JESSE GLOVER
(BRUCE LEE'S FIRST STUDENT)

(1) OBSERVING THE TEACHER

The young martial artist (Jesse Glover) sees his future teacher at the annual Seattle Seafair festival. The teacher (Bruce Lee) is then just a young college student, but Glover immediately recognizes the unique talents possessed by this master. Fortunately, the two are both students at Edison Technical College, where they will later meet.

(2) IMPRESSING THE TEACHER

The would-be student sees the teacher while walking to school one day. In order to get the teacher's attention, Glover runs ahead of Lee and begins kicking telephone poles as a demonstration of his might.

(3) THE MASTER AND THE STUDENT

The master, eager to share his knowledge, agrees to teach the student. At an early lesson, the student tries an attack on the teacher. The teacher effortlessly turns this attack around and forces the student to surrender. The student is both humbled and impressed.

4 A BOND IS FORMED

Glover and Lee have much knowledge to share
with each other, for that is the true nature of the
master-student bond: a collaborative union.
Together, they break with tradition and
advance the art of kung fu. And as the first of
Lee's students, Glover paves the way for many
future disciples and admirers.

5 THE MASTER MOVES ON

Bruce Lee, the great master, brings Chinese kung
fu—as well as his own form of martial arts, jeet kun
do—to the American public by becoming a film star.
In more than 20 films, the master demonstrates his
skill to an audience that has never before witnessed
anything like it. Although Lee dies at the young age
of 32, his legacy lives on as perhaps the most famous
martial artist of all time.

6 THE STUDENT'S LEGACY

As for the student, he is largely forgotten.
Even in the film biography of the master's
life, the student is portrayed as a somewhat
goofy amateur named Jerome Sprout. The
seriousness of Jesse's study and dedication
to kung fu are overlooked, as is his impact
on Bruce Lee's own kung fu style.

Lester Wunderman, Pioneer in "Direct Marketing"

(a.k.a. **JUNK MAIL**, **TELEMARKETING**, **TV INFOMERCIALS**, and **EMAIL SPAM**)

1952
Wunderman pushes a mail-order flower company's unwanted lavender plants by mailing unsolicited lavender-scented promo coupons to customers. $uccess!

1955
Wunderman helps Columbia Records launch a mail-order "record club," helping millions of Americans to accidentally spend too much on music.

1958
American Express consults Wunderman on its first-ever credit-card launch. He tells AmEx to call users "members" and charge a high annual fee.

So—
You know how sometimes, when you open up a magazine, it "automatically" opens to an ad on thicker paper? Guess who popularized that little trick.

Hey—
We don't think Lester Wunderman actually invented the magazine subscription card, but he's a big reason there are 87 of them in every magazine.

Dear **LESTER WUNDERMAN**,

Congratulations! In the cutthroat arena of **product advertising**, you're a **bonafide legend**. Your **talent** and **hard work** in the service of **esteemed corporate clients** brought you **financial wealth** and **professional distinction**.

LESTER -- In 1961, when you **coined the term "direct marketing"** to describe your set of **innovative, "personalized" advertising strategies**, you had **high hopes**. You envisioned a **gentler, more humane future** -- a future where **businesses** could share meaningful one-on-one **"dialogues"** with **every individual consumer**, just like the **good old days**.

In your view, America in the 1960s was "a **society in which human beings had become mere objects** in a system of **mass production** and **consumption**.... We [ad men] had forgotten **Immanuel Kant's warning** that **man** -- or in our case **customers** -- must be treated as an **end** and never a **means**."

You dreamed that the **personal touch** of **direct marketing** would lead to **better customer relationships**. Also: **way bigger profits. Profits up the wazoo!**

Nice dream, MR. WUNDERMAN. But we're **not sure** it's **worked out so well for the human race**. Thanks to you and your wayward disciples, **direct marketing** annoys us daily in the form of **junk mail**, **TV infomercials**, **telemarketing**, and **email spam!***

Sorry, LESTER WUNDERMAN. You're kind of a villain.

Best wishes,

This Book

---

* Direct marketing must generate massive profits -- but egads, man. Everyone alive hates it! The only thing worse than an "impersonal" advertisement is an advertisement that pretends to "know you" and "care." Ads like that are nauseating and intrusive, and the world would be better off without them. I think Mr. Kant is probably rolling in his grave!

In 1963, commercial artist Harvey Ball drew the world's first smiley face for an insurance company. The pins were an especially big hit, and the company gave away thousands of them. Soon, By 1971, more than 50 million smiley buttons had been sold. The smiley had become an "HAVE A NICE DAY!" to the smiley in the early 1970s, they grew richer than ever off the

in Massachusetts. The company made smiley pins and posters for its employees in order to lift spirits, and as a reminder to smile at customers.

numerous entrepreneurs—among them Bernard and Murray Spain of Philadelphia—began making and selling smiley products of their own. After the Spain brothers added the phrase

international symbol for peace and happiness, and would become one of the most popular images in the world.

borrowed symbol. Harvey Ball, who was paid $45 for creating the smiley and never saw a penny more, was said to have found that phrase "insipid."

SHAMU

(The original one)

The story of Shamu the killer whale (scientific name: Orcinus orca) is a complicated one. Of course, Shamu is hardly a forgotten hero. The performing whale is known and loved by millions for her inspired performances at Sea World. But anybody who has ever visited their grandparents in Florida has figured out that the Shamu you see at Sea World Orlando can't possibly be the same as the one you see at Sea World San Diego, right?* There are multiple whales performing under the stage name of Shamu. And in fact, there was only ever one original Shamu.

The Original Shamu began her stay at the San Diego Sea World in 1965. She was named after the first-ever performing killer whale, a male whale in Seattle named Namu. Shamu stands for "She-Namu."

Here's why things are complicated. When Shamu was taken from the wild, whale-trapping practices were crude and primitive, often resulting in the deaths of the whales. Shamu's own mother was killed in the process of catching Shamu. What's more, many whales have died while in captivity. The Original Shamu only lived for six years after she was captured. She died in 1971.

Conditions are better than they used to be at marine parks, but a great number of whales went to the big Sea World in the sky before things improved. The Original Shamu was one of those whales. It's important to consider the impact we have on our animal friends, especially when those animals are dying for our entertainment. We miss you, Original Shamu!

*Unless somebody is flying Shamu back and forth whenever you go see Nana and Pop-Pop, but that can't be right...

ROBERT PROPST

HE CALLED THE WORKPLACE A "WASTELAND" AND TRIED TO FIX IT— BUT THEN WHOOPS, HE INVENTED THE CUBICLE, WHICH MADE THINGS EVEN WORSE!

In the late 1940s, University of Colorado Fine Arts professor Robert Propst became a professional brainstormer. At work, he'd spend hours a day asking himself a simple question:

"How can I make life better?"

Propst came up with over 100 good answers to that question. Many of his life-improving ideas sound kind of dry—a quality-control system for concrete, for example—until you stop to think about them.*

In the 1950s, Propst called on Herman Miller, a popular furniture manufacturer, to present a new idea for connecting pieces of furniture to each other. Propst was hired, and he began to spend a great deal of time studying office workers and their work environments.

In 1960, Propst concluded that

"today's office is a wasteland. It saps vitality, blocks talent, frustrates accomplishment. It is the daily scene of unfulfilled intentions and failed effort."

Propst's answer was the Action Office—a whole new kind of walled furniture. It was a system of interlocking pieces that could be customized to meet workers' various and changing needs.

When Herman Miller launched the Action Office in 1968, Propst hoped it would promote health and enhance productivity. But sadly, this hope was crushed. Companies across the United States ordered heaps of the movable walls, constructing tiny little cubes and cramming them full of workers.

"They make little bitty cubicles and stuff people in them,"

Propst said, calling them

"barren, rat-hole places."

Robert Propst set out to make the average office a better place, but his accidental invention—the cubicle—has become the ultimate icon of workplace drudgery.

MONDAY

cubicles →

The Ack-tion Office

In the late '60s, Robert Propst's "Action Office" furniture system swept the country in a way that made Propst's hair stand on end.

Companies would buy the furniture, then construct cubicles in rows. These rows of cubicles were as bad as (or worse than) the rows of desks Propst was fighting against in the first place!

Today, companies around the world spend three billion dollars a year on cubicles.

* Personally, when we stop to think about all the concrete that surrounds us everywhere all the time, we are relieved that people like Robert Propst exist, and that they have spent serious time and energy thinking about the finer points of concrete production. As we sit here, now—in an underground parking garage in Columbus, Ohio—imagining a world in which all the concrete is less dependable, we feel intensely thankful to Mr. Propst. Our world may be a long way from perfect, but almost all the concrete we've used is solid and reliable and modestly heroic. Our lives would not be our lives without the overlooked greatness of well-made concrete. Thank you, Mr. Propst.

FAST FOOD

Maybe you're running late and you're hungry. There was a time when what to eat wouldn't even be an issue. Fast food was invented for just this sort of situation: busy days when you don't have time to cook a tasty, nourishing meal. Trouble is, fast food has gotten faster and less nourishing as the years go by. Everything from the french fries to the fish sandwich is loaded with fat and sugar, and eating too much can lead to any number of health problems, including heart disease, diabetes, and obesity. But the real problem may be just how big fast food meals have become.

Back in the 1950s, a man named David Wallerstein, who ran a series of movie theaters, found that he could sell more concessions to his moviegoers simply by increasing the size of his popcorn buckets and sodas to giganto-size. In 1968, he tried to convince McDonald's founder Ray Kroc to do the same with his food. Kroc didn't buy it. He thought that if people wanted more food, they'd just order more. But that's not the case. We Americans have an amazing ability to eat exactly how much food people give us, no matter how ridiculous the amount.

Wallerstein, of course, would eventually convince Kroc. The enormous baskets of fries and tubs of sodas we scarf down today were born. Other restaurants and businesses followed suit. It's safe to say that the great American weight problem is at least partly the fault of salesmen like David Wallerstein, but some of the blame rests on the fact that we just can't say no when somebody asks, "Do you want fries with that?" What should we do? Next time you get an order of fries, instead of thinking, "Look how many fries they gave me," maybe think, "Look how many fries they're making me eat!"

What's going on here, Lieutenant Calley?

What is this?
Who are these people?

Orders? Whose orders?

HUGH THOMPSON, JR.

was a United States Army helicopter pilot during the Vietnam War.

On March 16, 1968, while flying near the village of My Lai, he and his two companions noticed something strange. A group of U.S. soldiers appeared to be attacking Vietnamese civilians—mostly women, children, and the elderly—for no apparent reason.

Thompson landed the helicopter to take a closer look. He talked briefly with William Calley, one of the attackers. It was true: U.S. soldiers were killing unarmed Vietnamese. Thompson knew it had to stop.

He got back into the helicopter, lifted off, and landed between the attackers and a group of would-be victims. Then Thompson and his men took a big risk: they pointed their weapons at their fellow U.S. soldiers and ordered them to stop the killing.

Between 347 and 504 unarmed civilians died in the My Lai Massacre before the brave three-man intervention. The heroism of Hugh Thompson, Glenn Andreotta, and Lawrence Colburn wasn't officially recognized by the U.S. government until 1998.

But, these are human beings, unarmed civilians, sir.

Yeah, great job.

You ain't heard the last of this!

This is my business.

Just following orders.

Just following . . .

Look Thompson, this is my show.
I'm in charge here. It ain't your concern.

You better get back in that chopper and
mind your own business.

was the only U.S. Army officer to be convicted for participating in the 1968 My Lai Massacre. Twenty-five other soldiers were charged but not convicted.

Calley, who claimed he was merely following the orders of a commanding officer, was found guilty of multiple premeditated murders and sentenced to life in prison. But the day after the sentencing, President Richard Nixon transferred Calley from prison to house arrest at Fort Benning, Georgia.

Three and a half years later—on September 24, 1974—Calley was freed. The U.S. left Vietnam on April 30, 1975.

SPACE MAIL

Friends on Earth

1 Gravity Way

Anywhere, U.S.A.

Hi everyone,

Greetings from the Moon! We've both landed safely on the "Sea of Tranquility" on the lunar surface, and it is more ~~moon-y~~ amazing than we even thought possible. Unfortunately, Michael had to stay aboard the command module, and couldn't make it down to the Moon with us. But of course, he knew that coming in, and we couldn't have completed the mission without him. He's also in charge of piloting us back down to Earth safely. We think that he'll go down in history as the real hero of our trip. People will never forget his contributions to Apollo 11 as well as his work as co-captain of Gemini 10. His long history of service to his country and to the noble cause of space exploration should not be taken lightly. I just hope people won't forget about our small part in this voyage!

Yours truly,

Buzz and Neil

JOHN McCONNELL

founder of Earth Day

and a bona fide...

...GREEN CITIZEN

In 1939, John McConnell was working in plastics, when he had a crisis of conscience. Not many folks were worried about Mother Nature at the time, but McConnell was. He saw the effect plastic manufacturing had on the environment, and he understood the importance of raising awareness about the state of the Earth. Finally, in 1969, John McConnell proposed to the San Francisco Board of Supervisors that they set aside a day in celebration of the planet. The good folks of the Bay Area loved it.

But Earth Day was just one of numerous movements and causes that McConnell embraced. In 1957, he proposed the "Star of Hope," a joint U.S.-Soviet satellite he thought would encourage cooperation between the two nations. Then in 1962, there was "Meals for Millions," a program that helped feed thousands of Hong Kong refugees. Next up was "Minute for Peace." On December 22, 1963, radios and TVs across the country observed a moment of silence to mourn the death of President Kennedy, and usher in a new era of peace.

Only after all this did John come up with Earth Day. And after Earth Day's success in San Francisco, the United Nations caught wind. On March 21, 1970, at the moment of the March Equinox, the United Nations rang the Peace Bell and Earth Day was proclaimed. The tradition of Earth Day continues to this day, with the continuing hope that, when the Peace Bell rings each year, we will forget our differences and think of what we have in common: a beautiful planet that needs our care.

"Whenever I nee uncontrollably up a world withou

Before all the Xboxes, Nintendos, and Playstations, there were Segas and more Nintendos. And before that, there were Ataris, Intellivisions, and Commodore 64s.

And before that, there were video arcades full of games you could play for a quarter. Games like Space Invaders, Pac-Man, and Donkey Kong—the timeless classics your forefathers enjoyed.

And before all that, there was Pong—the first arcade video game to sweep the nation. Pong was a two-player ping-pong game, and in the early 1970s, people couldn't get enough. The USA had Pong fever!

Mario

JAYSON FRANKLIN, AN EIGHT-YEAR-OLD VIDEO-GAME ENTHUSIAST FROM TOLEDO, OHIO:

d to make myself
set, I just imagine
t video games."

Because Pong was so popular, it's often remembered as "the first video game." But that's just not correct. Before Pong, there was the Magnavox Odyssey—the very first video-game machine of them all.

Ralph Baer, an electrical engineer, started designing the Odyssey in 1966, and it was released in 1972. The Odyssey could play several games on any TV, including a tennis game that was copied by the makers of Pong. (They later apologized.) Baer also invented the video-game light gun.

Without Ralph Baer, the video game as we know it might not exist.

hedgehog

PATSY T. MINK AND TITLE IX

Patsy Takemoto Mink was the first Japanese-American woman to be elected to the United States Congress. Between 1965 and 2002 Mink served two terms as a representative from her home state of Hawaii—once from 1965 to 1977 and the other from 1991 until her death in 2002. Early childhood encounters with inequality between white and non-white Hawaiian residents instilled Mink with a lifelong belief in creating equal opportunities for all people. Throughout her time in Congress, she served with a defiant approach to those who would oppose the rights of others. When she felt strongly about an issue, she was not afraid to take an unpopular stand. Perhaps most memorably, in 1972 she co-sponsored and authored a piece of legislation known as Title IX. Title IX prohibits discrimination based on gender in any education programs that receive federal money. One issue that Title IX addresses is women's participation in sports. Because of Mink's piece of legislation, colleges and high schools are required to provide equal funding and opportunities to both men's and women's sports. Without Title IX, some of the greatest American athletes may never have had the opportunity to hone their skills, let alone get into college. So while Patsy never won the trophies and awards that the women on these pages did, she was a true champion of women's sports.

JUST A FEW RIDICULOUSLY TALENTED AMERICAN WOMEN

Use this key to learn about the women shown on the opposite page.

1. PATSY MINK
You know who she is. Just read the above section!

2. WILMA RUDOLPH, TRACK
Wilma's three Olympic gold medals came before Title IX, but her amazing story deserves mention. She overcame pneumonia, scarlet fever, and polio to become one of the greatest runners of all time.

3. LAILA ALI, BOXING
The daughter of one of the greatest boxers of all time, Muhammad Ali, Laila managed to step out of her father's shadow—while following in his footsteps to succeed in a sport dominated by men.

4. MIA HAMM, SOCCER
One of the greatest soccer players of all time, Hamm put U.S. soccer on the map, and inspired a generation of young soccer players.

5. JACKIE JOYNER-KERSEE, TRACK
Jackie Joyner-Kersee was one of the greatest products of Title IX. She excelled in the heptathlon, and won six Olympic medals (1988–1996). Her path to greatness is admired and followed by athletes in all sports.

6. BILLIE JEAN KING, TENNIS
King won 39 Grand Slams, and 695 matches overall, but most importantly, she is a true leader of the women's athletics movement. She fought tirelessly for equal prize money for women, and in 1973, a year after the passage of Title IX, she soundly beat Bobby Riggs in a legendary "Battle of the Sexes."

7. LISA LESLIE, BASKETBALL
Leslie translated a stellar collegiate career into great success in the WNBA, helping to put professional women's basketball on the map.

8. PICABO STREET, SKIING
With a captivating personality and real grit, Street overcame injuries to win gold in the 1998 Winter Olympics, and pave the way for female skiers and snowboarders.

9. MARY LOU RETTON, GYMNASTICS
At only 4'9" tall and 92 lbs (41.7 kg), Retton still stood tall. In 1984, she became the first American woman to win an Olympic medal (of any kind) in gymnastics.

10. NATALIE COUGHLIN, SWIMMING
Coughlin represents the new generation of female athletes. After competing for UC Berkeley, she set a record in 2008 by winning six Olympic medals in Beijing.

11. JENNIE FINCH, SOFTBALL
One of the greatest to ever play one of the most popular collegiate sports.

HURRAH FOR BARCODES!

ESPECIALLY THE

UPC†

TA-DA! ⟶   ⟵ WOO-HOO!

1 23456 78910 4

(UNIVERSAL PRODUCT CODE†)

"Helping everybody save time and money in the checkout line since 1974.*"

*On June 26, 1974, a pack of chewing gum became the first item ever sold with the help of a UPC barcode. This historic event took place in a supermarket in Troy, Ohio. Now, around the world, the UPC and more than 300 other types of barcode are now scanned by barcode readers billions of times every day.

THE INVENTORS!

In 1948, two young engineers named Joseph Woodland and Bernard Silver invented the barcode. Their goal was simple: to create an automated system that could keep track of every item sold in a supermarket.

THE EUREKA MOMENT!

The basic structure of barcodes flew into Woodland's head while he was at the beach. He started drawing the dots and dashes of Morse code in the sand (fig. 1) and then extended those marks into lines (fig. 2). Woodland knew that a liney pattern like this could store key information about a grocery item, like its price. The info stored in the line pattern could then be "read" by a machine using a strong light.

fig. 1

THE LOOOOOONG WAIT FOR LASER LIGHT!

After his beach breakthrough, all Woodland had to do next was wait about 20 years for the right kind of light—a light that could easily read barcodes. After cheap lasers became available in the early '70s, the humble UPC barcode finally made a big supermarket splash!

fig. 2

CHEAPER LIVING THROUGH BARCODES!

In just a few decades, the UPC barcode has helped America save billions of dollars on groceries alone. Without the UPC barcode, the price of groceries would have risen twice as fast since the '70s!

FASTER LIVING THROUGH BARCODES!

In the several seconds it takes to ring up a grocery item by hand, about ten items can be rung up using a barcode scanner. So the next time you're stuck standing in a grocery checkout line, spend a moment thanking barcodes. Without them, you'd be waiting in line a lot longer.

The UPC barcode, which was the world's first widely successful barcode, was developed in the early '70s by a team of IBM engineers including George Laurer. Like all barcode designs, the UPC barcode owes its basic structure to Woodland and Silver. Aren't you glad Woodland went to the beach?

We now present the gutsy, nervy, David-and-Goliath-like story of . . .

MICHAEL LARSON

THE UNEMPLOYED ICE-CREAM TRUCK DRIVER
from LEBANON, OHIO *who* OUTSMARTED A TV NETWORK
to become the BIGGEST ONE-DAY WINNER *in* GAME-SHOW HISTORY

Lebanon

ON A SPRING DAY IN 1984 . . .
Michael Larson won $110,237 in cash and prizes on the CBS game show *Press Your Luck.*
That's more than triple the amount anyone had ever won in a full week on the show,
and more money than anybody had ever won on any game show in one day.

HOW DID HE WIN SO BIG ???

WARNING: FINE PRINT. MAY REQUIRE EXTREME, MICHAEL-LARSON-LIKE CONCENTRATION.

It's simple, kind of. *Press Your Luck* was supposed to be a random-chance button-pressing game, but it ended up not being random. There were patterns, and those patterns could be exploited.

Here's how the game works: There are 18 squares on a big board. At any moment, one square is lit. You try to stop the jumping light when it's on a "prize" square. But watch out! You might stop the light on a "Whammy" square instead. If you hit a Whammy, you lose all your prize money and your turn ends.

If you hit a prize square, you generally

have two options: (1) take another "spin" and hope you *don't* hit a Whammy, or (2) pass your remaining spins to another player and hope they *do* hit a Whammy. The player with the most prize money at the end wins.

By taping and rewatching dozens of *Press Your Luck* episodes on his VCR (a new technology at the time), Michael Larson figured out the game's light patterns. (There were only five!) Larson studied these patterns and used the "pause" button on his VCR remote to perfect his light-stopping technique.

Once he had it down pat, Larson borrowed money for a plane ticket to LA, where he bought a 65¢ button-down shirt from a thrift store and successfully auditioned for the show.

On the show, Larson went to town, winning over $100,000 on a single turn.

Average contestants would hit a Whammy within two or three spins. It was considered very lucky to go five spins in a row without hitting a Whammy. Michael Larson took 40 consecutive spins without hitting a Whammy, then stopped.

SHOCKED HOST!

The host of *Press Your Luck*, Peter Tomarken, was astonished by Michael Larson's incredibly "lucky" performance. Only after the show's taping did Tomarken and CBS figure out that Larson had discovered patterns in the "random" game board.

For the last 30 minutes of Larson's unprecedented 40-spin Whammy-free turn, Tomarken's face was pretty much frozen in this expression.

NO WHAMMIES!

A typical Whammy square looked like this.
If Larson had hit just one of these squares on the way to $110,237, he would have gone back to $0.

Good thing he'd practiced dodging Whammies at home with that VCR remote!

CHEATER? NO WAY!

After CBS discovered Michael Larson's Whammy-dodging method, the station hoped to brand him a cheater and void all his winnings.

In the end, CBS decided it couldn't legally prove that Larson had cheated. He'd simply *beaten the game*.

Larson walked away with all $110,237, and CBS quietly reconfigured its game board.

BUT...

Sadly, Michael Larson lost everything he won not long after his performance aired on TV.

A real-estate Ponzi scheme swallowed most of the winnings. Larson withdrew the rest — roughly $40,000 — in one-dollar bills, hoping to win a local radio contest in which a random serial number was announced over the air. The contest offered thousands of dollars to anyone who could produce a one-dollar bill matching the announced number.

The briefcase containing Larson's $40,000 in ones was swiped during a Christmas party. Michael Larson, a tragic hero, died nearly penniless in 1999.

THE TEENAGE

MARY

Four-year-old Mary Rodas used to help her father out as he made repairs to the apartment building where they lived. Her father had come from El Salvador and worked hard to make a life for himself and his daughter in America. He wanted Mary to pursue the American Dream, to work hard and rise from humble beginnings.

TOY TYCOON

RODAS

Lucky for Mary, she wouldn't have to wait too long. Living in the same building as the Rodas family was a man by the name of Don Spector, a toymaker, who was in need of a kid's opinion. Lucky for Don, Mary was more than willing to share hers, and, as it turns out, she had an unbelievably keen eye for which toys would work and which toys would flop.

NOTE: When Mary finished elementary school, Spector made her the vice president of his company, Catco Toys. A few days a week, Mary would take a limo to Catco headquarters after school, so she could offer her opinions on the latest products. Pretty cool job, right? Well, Mary did it well, and before she went to college, she had already gone from the daughter of a poor immigrant to a very young, very wealthy executive.

REAL ESTATE

The Daily American Hero

June 4, 2007

From Science Experiment to Retirement Home?

Attention home buyers! This stunning 3.14-acre scientific research compound in the Sonoran Desert might just be your ticket to owning a piece of Arizona real estate with heroic potential.

ORACLE, Arizona — The property has more than seven million cubic feet of glass in 6,500 windows. It includes a private ocean with coral reef, mangrove wetlands, tropical rainforest, savannah grassland, and fog desert.

You could own it all, if you're willing to pay a hefty price!

The building in question is Biosphere 2. Built in the 1980s, the enormous glass structure lies in the middle of the Sonoran desert, between Phoenix and Tuscon, Arizona. It was built to house a $200-million experiment in survival, recycling, ecosystems, and human interaction.

On Friday, September 27, 1991, eight brave men and women, dressed in blue jumpsuits— Abigail Alling, Roy Walford, Jane Poynter, Linda Leigh, Taber McCallum, Sally Silverstone, Mark Nelson, and Mark Van Taillo— entered Biosphere 2, where they had all agreed to live for two years, without any assistance from the outside world.

Inside were thousands of plants and animals, placed within to simulate a small version of the Earth (the first Biosphere). The "Bionauts" would raise their own food, conduct experiments, and have minimal contact with the outside world.

It was all planned out like a science fiction movie. How could it get any more incredible? A privately funded project in a remote location. An oasis in the desert. Scientists removed from the entire world around them. People were fascinated! Could humans live like this? Could we build one of these on the Moon? Mars? The possibilities were endless.

Then oxygen started running out inside. Ants and insects began to take over. The ocean became acidic. Crops failed.

A couple of the residents were caught breaking the Biosphere's seals. It was then revealed that food and supplies were being smuggled inside. The "Bionauts" were not living as they had intended.

Another mission launched in 1994 tried to recapture the magic of the first voyage, but never really succeeded.

In the years following the Biosphere projects, the nearby cities of Phoenix and Tucson expanded outwardly, growing ever closer to the Biosphere. The location was growing less and less remote as homes and shopping malls popped up closer and closer.

By 2005, offers were coming in from real estate developers interested in buying up the Biosphere property and the surrounding land. Was this once noble experiment about to become a suburban tract of retirement homes? Developers were throwing around the name "Biosphere Estates."

In 2007, a company called CDO Ranching & Development bought the Biosphere for a quarter of what it cost to build. The plan was to build a series of homes, hotels, and stores on the land.

Fortunately, the University of Arizona stepped up and decided to lease the Biosphere to conduct experiments. But experiments need funding, and in all likelihood, the Biosphere is bound to become nothing more than a futuristic-looking park in the middle of a normal neighborhood.

But for a brief time in history, it was something special! Inside Biosphere 2, men and women lived surrounded by its glass walls, suspended from reality, with endless possibilities ahead.

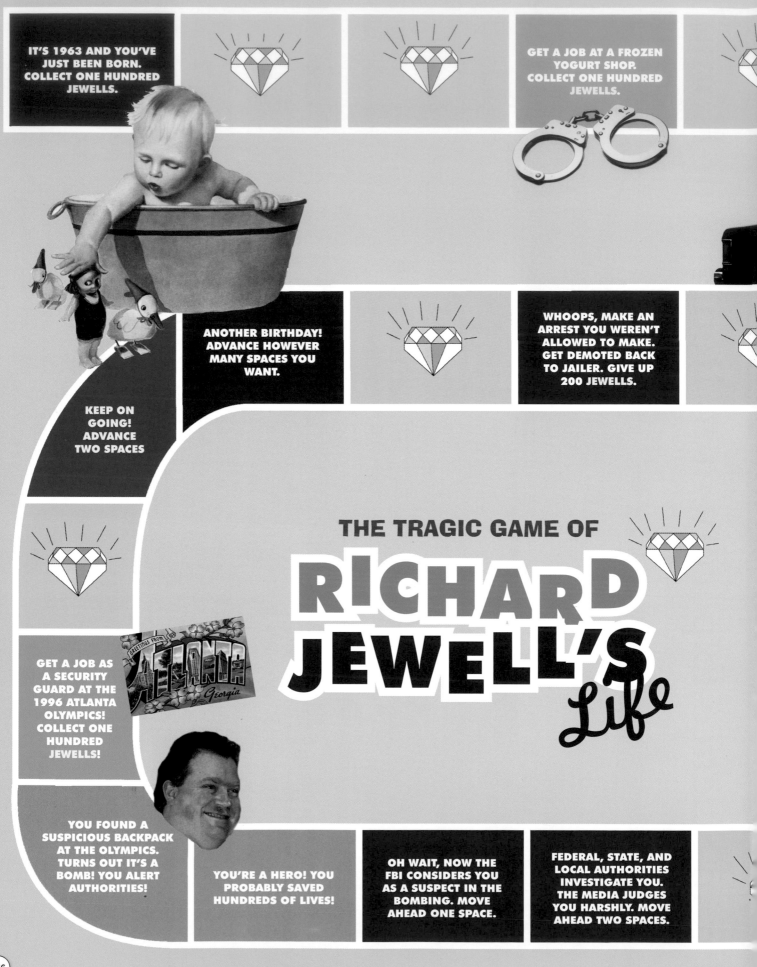

THE TRAGIC GAME OF

RICHARD JEWELL'S Life

IT'S 1963 AND YOU'VE JUST BEEN BORN. COLLECT ONE HUNDRED JEWELLS.

GET A JOB AT A FROZEN YOGURT SHOP. COLLECT ONE HUNDRED JEWELLS.

ANOTHER BIRTHDAY! ADVANCE HOWEVER MANY SPACES YOU WANT.

WHOOPS, MAKE AN ARREST YOU WEREN'T ALLOWED TO MAKE. GET DEMOTED BACK TO JAILER. GIVE UP 200 JEWELLS.

KEEP ON GOING! ADVANCE TWO SPACES

GET A JOB AS A SECURITY GUARD AT THE 1996 ATLANTA OLYMPICS! COLLECT ONE HUNDRED JEWELLS!

YOU FOUND A SUSPICIOUS BACKPACK AT THE OLYMPICS. TURNS OUT IT'S A BOMB! YOU ALERT AUTHORITIES!

YOU'RE A HERO! YOU PROBABLY SAVED HUNDREDS OF LIVES!

OH WAIT, NOW THE FBI CONSIDERS YOU AS A SUSPECT IN THE BOMBING. MOVE AHEAD ONE SPACE.

FEDERAL, STATE, AND LOCAL AUTHORITIES INVESTIGATE YOU. THE MEDIA JUDGES YOU HARSHLY. MOVE AHEAD TWO SPACES.

GET A JOB AS A PRIVATE DETECTIVE. COLLECT ONE HUNDRED JEWELLS.

SORT OF JUST LIVING A NORMAL LIFE, MORE OR LESS. ADVANCE FOUR SPACES.

IT'S YOUR BIRTHDAY! MOVE AHEAD TWO SPACES

GET A PROMOTION TO SQUAD-CAR DEPUTY. COLLECT ONE HUNDRED JEWELLS.

GET A JOB AS A JAILER IN GEORGIA. COLLECT ONE HUNDRED JEWELLS.

YUP, LIFE IS MOVING ALONG PRETTY REGULARLY. ADVANCE ONE SPACE.

The tragic story of Richard Jewell demonstrates what happens when people—law enforcement, the media, you, me—jump to conclusions too soon. Even after he was cleared of suspicion, Jewell continued to suffer from the negative association he had been given. He tried to sue the media outlets that wrongfully portrayed him as the bomber, but not much came of it. And so, lost in all the rumors and lies was the simple fact that Richard Jewell did a very brave thing and saved many lives.

SOMEONE REFERRED TO YOU AS THE "UNA-DOOFUS," AND MANY HAVE DEEMED YOU GUILTY.

IN 2005, ERIC R. RUDOLPH IS CONVICTED OF THE BOMBING. YOUR NAME IS CLEARED! MOVE AHEAD ONE SPACE.

YOU NEVER QUITE ESCAPE THE POOR PUBLICITY. YOU SUE THE NEWS NETWORKS, BUT NOT MUCH COMES OF IT SADLY.

YOU PASS AWAY IN 2007. THIS BOOK RECOGNIZES YOU AS A TRUE HERO, THOUGH!

Marty Ravellette

Marty Ravellette was born without arms in Indiana in 1939. His parents, not knowing how to deal with his rare handicap, sent him to live in an orphanage. Before long, Ravellette was gripping the baby bottle with his feet and feeding himself. "That was the start," he'd say, "of learning to do things myself."

As a boy, Ravellette loved to swim, and won diving medals. Later, he worked as a truck driver, steering with his left foot and pressing the pedals with his right. (When you're as good as Marty Ravellette, this is legal.) He traveled all over the country and tried all kinds of things—construction, coaching softball, getting married, raising kids, custodial work—before settling in Chapel Hill, North Carolina in 1991 and starting his own business: "Hands On Landscaping." His business card made people laugh: it included a picture of two feet.

He embraced life—
and even saved a couple lives—
with zero arms on his body.

Funny, hard-working, and armless, Ravellette became a local legend. He once used a chainsaw—his so-called "favorite tool"—to cut up a fallen tree in the middle of a hurricane. Another time, he received a thank-you letter from a man who had been thinking about killing himself. When the man drove by Ravellette—who was pushing a lawnmower with his chest under the hot sun, sweat pouring—he decided to keep living, even though life was hard.

To top it all off, Marty Ravellette and his wife Maree rescued a woman from her burning car in 1998. Using his feet to break the window, Ravellette saved the woman seconds before the wrecked car burst into flames. The woman called Ravellette an "angel without wings," and Ravellette began delivering lectures to students, emphasizing the importance of accepting all people, no matter how different they might seem. When people asked Marty Ravellette if he wished he had arms, he always told them no. "I am what I am today because I don't have arms. And I like who I am."

Marty Ravellette died in 2007.

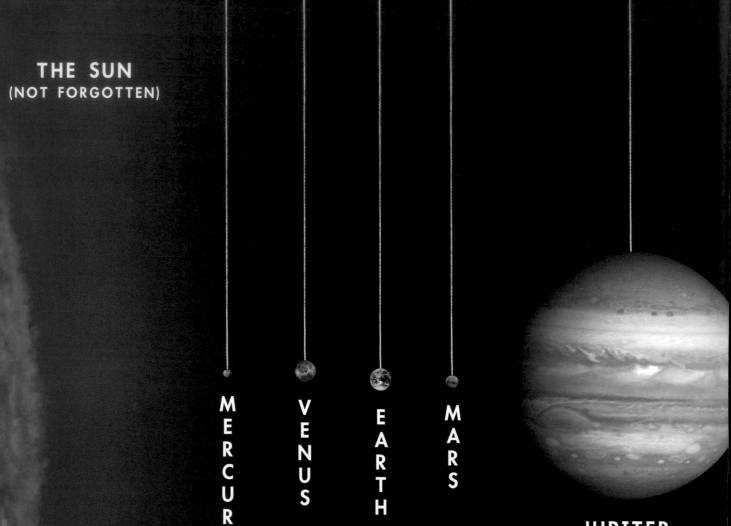

THE SUN
(NOT FORGOTTEN)

M
E
R
C
U
R
Y

V
E
N
U
S

E
A
R
T
H

M
A
R
S

JUPITER

For seventy-six years, Pluto was considered the ninth planet of our solar system. First sighted in 1930, it was also the only planet discovered by American scientists. Clyde W. Tombaugh of Lowell Observatory in Arizona stumbled upon Pluto while searching for the mysterious-sounding Planet X, which scientists believed was causing the orbit of Neptune to act strangely. Pluto isn't Planet X—there is no Planet X—but it was pretty cool to have discovered a ninth planet anyway. Pluto even has a moon, Charon, which was discovered by another American astronomer, James Christy, in 1978.

Pluto held its place as the ninth—and smallest—planet until 2006, when the International Astronomical Union downgraded it to a "dwarf planet." How rude! According to those IAU sticks-in-the-mud, in order to be a planet, Pluto must 1) orbit the Sun, 2) be big enough for gravity to squash it into a round ball, and 3) have cleared other things out of the way in its space neighborhood. Rule number three is what disqualifies Pluto. That's right. As easy as that, the only "American" planet is now no longer a planet. Generations to come will learn about the eight planets in our solar system, but some of us will always remember PLUTO: THE NINTH PLANET.

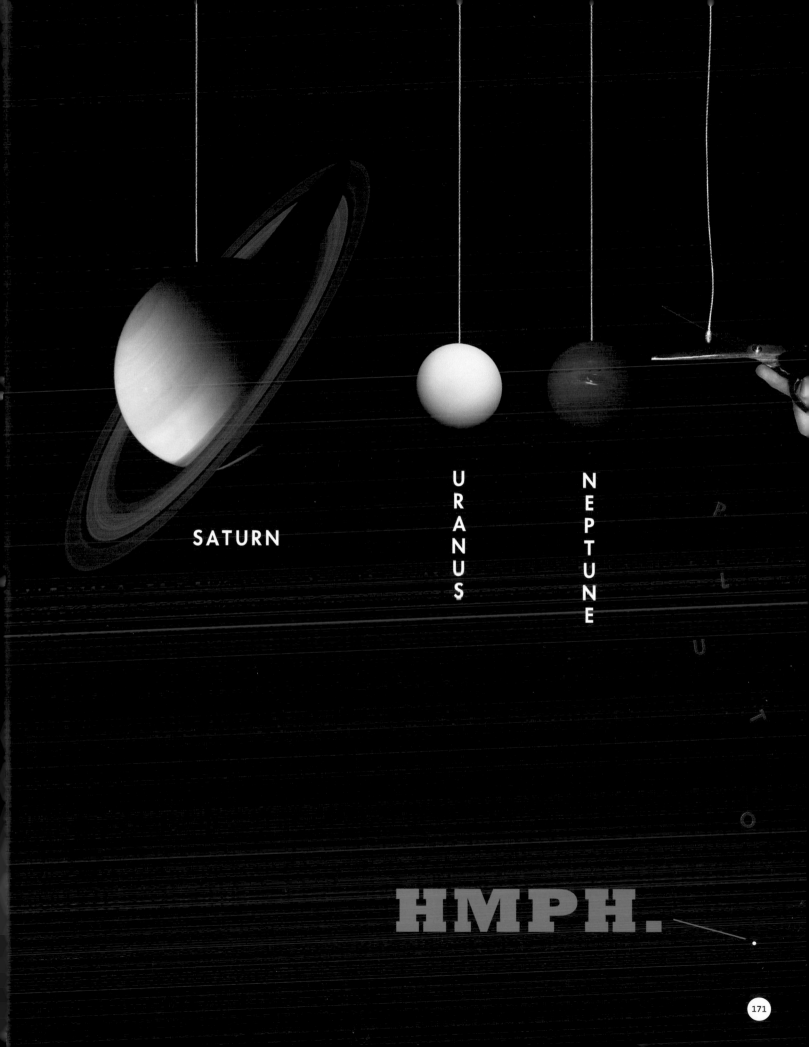

SATURN

URANUS

NEPTUNE

PLUTO

HMPH.

THE ONCE MIGHTY AND NOW FORGOTTEN
BERTHA*

*The name Bertha, not necessarily a specific Bertha

One of the few modern Americans given the glorious and all-but-forgotten name Bertha.

What Happened to Bertha?

What happened to Bertha? Why did American parents stop naming their babies Bertha? The name Bertha has been in rapid and steady decline for 120 years (as long as the Social Security Administration has been keeping track of these things). Perhaps, it was the BIG BERTHA—a German cannon that became well-known during World War I—that turned people sour on Bertha. What else could it have been? Bertha is such a fascinating name (it comes from the German word for "bright")! It's sad to think of how many American heroes have been named Sally, or Cathy, or Margaret, or Fiona, while just because someone nicknamed a gun Bertha, all the nice, decent Berthas of America got a bad rap. It's unfair, really. Below is a graph demonstrating the tragic fall of Bertha in America.

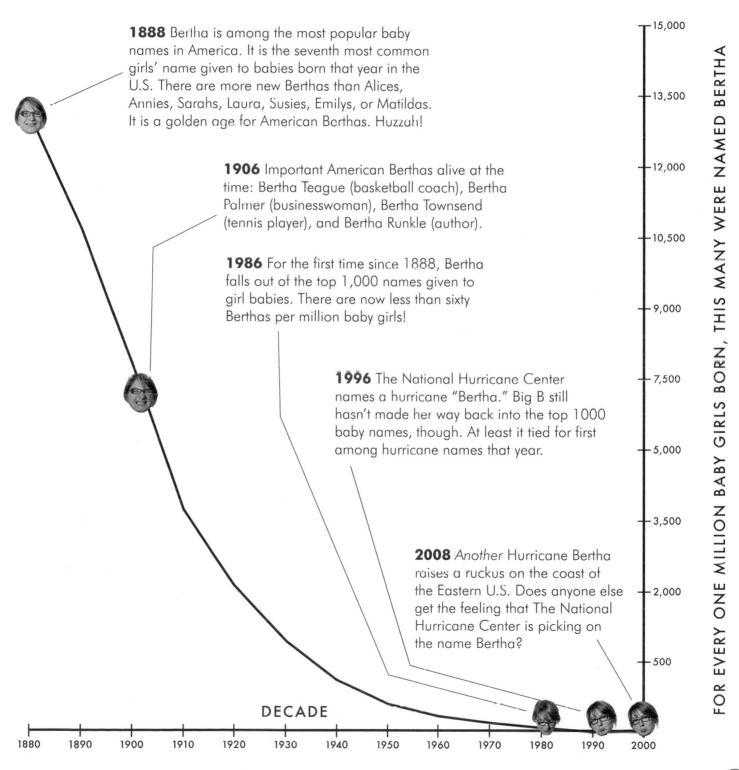

1888 Bertha is among the most popular baby names in America. It is the seventh most common girls' name given to babies born that year in the U.S. There are more new Berthas than Alices, Annies, Sarahs, Laura, Susies, Emilys, or Matildas. It is a golden age for American Berthas. Huzzah!

1906 Important American Berthas alive at the time: Bertha Teague (basketball coach), Bertha Palmer (businesswoman), Bertha Townsend (tennis player), and Bertha Runkle (author).

1986 For the first time since 1888, Bertha falls out of the top 1,000 names given to girl babies. There are now less than sixty Berthas per million baby girls!

1996 The National Hurricane Center names a hurricane "Bertha." Big B still hasn't made her way back into the top 1000 baby names, though. At least it tied for first among hurricane names that year.

2008 Another Hurricane Bertha raises a ruckus on the coast of the Eastern U.S. Does anyone else get the feeling that The National Hurricane Center is picking on the name Bertha?

DECADE

1880 1890 1900 1910 1920 1930 1940 1950 1960 1970 1980 1990 2000

FOR EVERY ONE MILLION BABY GIRLS BORN, THIS MANY WERE NAMED BERTHA

15,000
13,500
12,000
10,500
9,000
7,500
5,000
3,500
2,000
500

TIM GERSTMANN (WASHINGTON)

...respects his parents. They are both older and are struggling to live life on their own. He knows that living in their house in Puyallup, WA, and being able to do their church activities throughout the week is important to them. Every weekend he cooks meals for them and does any shopping they might need. He takes care of their broken stove and the loose tiles in the bathroom, changes light bulbs, and brings them embarrassingly large packages of adult diapers without batting an eye.

PAM CHUTE (MONTANA)

...was driving her boat along Swan Lake when she spotted a soda bottle floating in the water. Picking it up, she realized it had a hook and bait attached. She then noticed a dozen more floating-bottle fish traps that some lazy person had thrown in the lake in order to catch the biggest fish. Worried this illegal, polluting practice would deplete the lake of vital fish, she pulled the bottles from the water.

LARA DENNELLI PETICLERC (OREGON)

...of Baker City shoveled snow off of her sidewalk and the sidewalks of three of her neighbors.

MAGGIE MATCHIN (CALIFORNIA)

... Maggie is an HIV-test counselor for homeless youth in San Francisco. Every day she walks all around the city and talks to kids about HIV/AIDS, administers tests, and helps them understand and cope with the results. Maggie knows everything there is to know about HIV/AIDS, and she spends her days sharing her knowledge with other people so that they can protect themselves. She is incredibly smart and brave, and always wants to help people.

AARON REYNOLDS (TEXAS)

...is an artist in Austin. In his spare time, he teaches painting to young people who are incarcerated at Gardner Betts Juvenile Justice Center.

EVERYDAY FORGOTTEN AMERICAN HEROES

MONICA LAMS (MICHIGAN)

...is a nightshift waitress at the Fleetwood Diner in Ann Arbor. After serving her 10,000th rude customer and receiving a meager tip, she did not lose her smile. Then, at dawn, when all the tables were wiped down, she stayed an extra 20 minutes to help regular morning customer Joe Donovan, 77, a resident of the men's shelter down the street, complete a crossword puzzle.

ALEX CARP (NEW YORK)

...was leaving the F Train station on 2nd Ave. in New York City, when he saw a woman struggling to carry her baby carriage (with baby on board) up the stairs. Other commuters just passed by, but Alex stopped and asked the woman if she needed a hand. She smiled and said yes. Alex waved at the baby, picked up the front of the carriage and helped the woman up the stairs.

JIM WALKER (INDIANA)

...of Indianapolis puts his children Vivien and Max to bed every night, lifting his 8-year-old daughter up to her top bunk even though it hurts his back. Then he reads to them so his wife can relax.

JORDAN AINSLEY (GEORGIA)

...of Atlanta took pity on an abused and neglected pit bull named Alice. Jordan rescued her and fed her. A few weeks later, Alice took a bite of Jordan's arm, but Jordan still let her stay at her house until she found a proper home for Alice.

RACHAEL STODARD AND STACEY LEE (LOUISIANA)

...stopped their car on the side of the road to help upright a turtle who had fallen on his back while trying to climb a curb.

INDEX

Thank you.

Drew Altizer	Billie Jean	Lindsay Quella
Josiah Bartlett	Julia Kinsman	Michelle Quint
Jordan Bass	Nicholas Koch	Rhea's Deli & Grocery
Bob & Lynn Burress	Andrew Leland	Gabe Robinson
Jimmy Calhoun	Juliet Litman	Davy Rothbart
Alex Carp	Lauren LoPrete	Onnesha Roychoudhuri
Ira Chute	Mary Lowry	San Francisco Public Library
DK Publishing	Alex Ludlum	David Serlin
Jay Dickason	Pete Mack	Chris Sheehy
Dave Eggers	Ted Mallison	Tanya Sirkin
Matt Furie	Shauta Marsh	Rachael Stodard
Margaret Gadwohl	Aric Mayer	Perry Stokes
Kimberlee Gerstmann	Katie & Alton McMullen	Tess Thackara
Tim Gough	Heidi Meredith	Nicholas Thomson
Joanna Green	Mary Kay Mosby	Eric Vennemeyer
Eli Horowitz	Jesse Nathan	Werner
Ian Huebert	Kyle O'Loughlin	Jami Witek
Renae Hurlbutt	Angela Petrella	Jayme Yen

With special grateful feelings for the following publications:

Banvard's Folly, Paul Collins
A People's History of the United States, Howard Zinn
That's Not in My American History Book, Thomas Ayres
The Greatest Stories Never Told, Rick Beyer
Cabinet magazine
The Believer

The authors and the publisher would like to thank the following individuals and institutions for their kind permission to reproduce their original artwork, photographs, and other images in this book.

(Key: a-above; b-below/bottom; c-center; f-far; l-left; r-right; t-top)

Amelia Bauer: 128–129 (Brownie Wise); **Jimmy Calhoun:** 160–161 (all drawings); **Matt Furie:** We're bummed in the extreme that we couldn't use your amazing painting of all the video-game characters. We owe you one. Meanwhile, we've framed and hung the painting on our wall, and it'll stay there for the rest of our life. **Tim Gough:** 132–133 (Claudette Colvin), 136–137 (all drawings); **Ian Huebert:** 4–5 (George Robert Twelves Hewes), 12–13 (Sarah Tarrant), 92–93 (Stephen Mather); **Billie Jean:** 1 (Deganawidah), 168–169 (Marty Ravellette).

Aric Mayer: 79 (cereal bowl) 80–81 (Hero Sandwich); **Corbis:** 89c, 150c (Earth); Buzz Aldrin 150c (Neil Armstrong); Marilyn Angel Wynn / Nativestock Pictures / Corbis Encyclopedia 24bl; M. Angelo 130; Neil Armstrong 150c (Buzz Aldrin), 150c (flag); Neil Armstrong / Bettman 150c (lunar module); Rick Barrentine 134-135; Annie Griffiths Belt 102-103; Bettmann 18, 32b, 50-51, 51cr, 55bl, 55c, 56tl, 61br, 74tr, 75bc, 75tc, 86cb, 87bl, 87tr, 100cla, 108-109, 116, 117, 119b, 124, 125bc, 148, 149, 150c (Apollo 11), 150c (command module), 150c (moon), 156cl, 156cla; Bettmann / Underwood & Underwood 106-107; Blue Lantern Studio 72c, 166clb, 166tl; Blue Lantern Studio / Corbis Art 57tr; Burke / Triolo Productions / Brand X 30bc; Tami Chappell / Reuters 167br; Rob Chatterson / Corbis Yellow 29tc; Mike Chick / Zefa 98-99; Edward S. Curtis / Christie's Images 66; David J. & Janice L. Frent Collection 150c (pin); Elements / CSA Images 62bc; Fancy / Veer 19; Deborah Feingold 154br; Greg Fiume / NewSport 156br; Tom Grill / Corbis Yellow 29cb; Masashi Hayasaka / Amanaimages 62bl, 62br; Chris Hellier 65bl; Historical 44tc; Rainer Holz / zefa 167ca; Gary Houlder 143; Dick Kitchen / Bettmann 107c; Justin Lane / epa 156c; William Manning / Terra 30-31; Vince Mannino / Bettmann 107bc; James Marshall 164; moodboard 166tr; Lucy Nicholson / Reuters 156tl; Gerry Penny / epa 165tl; Charles Platiau / Reuters 156ca; Neal Preston 156tc; Printstock / CSA Images 86tc, 145tr; William Radcliffe / Science Faction 154-155; Reuters 156cr, 165tc; H. Armstrong Roberts 145tl; Lew Robertson / Corbis Yellow 21tr, 29crb; Benjamin Rondel 94c; Ariel Skelley 164tr; Philip Spruyt / Stapleton Collection 56bl; Brian David Stevens 34-35; Scott Stulberg 90bl; Noeru Takizawa / Amanaimages 98-99 (bulb); Hiroshi Teshigawara / amanaimages 155br; Chris Trotman / Duomo 156tr; Universal / TempSport 156bl; Bill Varie 144-145; **Getty Images:** Burazin 48tr; C Squared Studios 138; Alex Cao 23ca; Doug Collier / AFP 166bl; Jeffrey Coolidge / Digital Vision 57cr; Antar Dayal 55br, 55crb, 55fcrb; Macduff Everton 1; Foodcollection 146-147; John Foxx / Stockbyte 29clb; Hulton Archive 55fclb, 129; Hulton Archive / MPI 55fbl; Hulton Archive / Stock Montage 54c, 55clb; Daniel Hurst 40; Russell Kaye / Sandra-Lee Phipps 165tr; Keystone / Hulton Archive 123; Robert Laberge 156cb; Mansell / Time & Life Pictures 94-95; George Marks / Hulton Archive 121crb (forehead reflector); MPI / Hulton Archive 50cl; Photodisc 31br; Photographer's Choice / Richard Ross 26; Siede Preis / Photodisc 56-57; Roger Ressmeyer / NASA 150cb; Paul J. Richards / AFP 95br; Lew Robertson / Photographer's Choice 29bc, 29bl, 29br, 29ca, 29cla (cone), 29cra; George Rose 125c; Stockbyte 24-25 (Hands); StockFood Creative / John Kelly 22bc, 23br; Nic Taylor / iStock Exclusive 26; Paul Taylor / The Image Bank 29tr; Time Life Pictures / Mansell 54bl; Hank Walker / Time & Life Pictures 120crb, 121crb; ©2009 Jupiterimages Corporation: 72-73; **Library Of Congress, Washington, D.C.:** 23bc, 24-25c, 59crb; **Alfie Moon:** 112; **NASA:** 126-127, 127c, 170-171; **The US National Archives and Records Administration:** Record Group 360 21clb, 21crb

Jacket images: *Front:* **Corbis:** Bettmann bl (Christopher Latham Sholes), cb (Josh Gibson), clb (Edwin H. Land), clb (Molly Pitcher), fbr (Nellie Bly); Mike Chick / Zefa fcr (braids); Edward S. Curtis / Christie's Images crb (Chief Joseph); Noeru Takizawa / Amanaimages fcr (bulb); **Getty Images:** Time Life Pictures / Mansell cr (Charles Francis Adams); © **2009 Jupiterimages Corporation:** fcrb (elephant). *Front Flaps:* **Corbis:** Bettmann br; *Back Endpapers:* **Corbis:** Frank Ebeling / Zefa

All other images © Dorling Kindersley
For further information see: www.dkimages.com

THE END

Dear Trees,

We'd like to take a moment, back here, to thank those of you who gave up your lives in the service of this book. You may not have been born in the United States— which means you were never eligible to run for president— but the USA is where we've arranged for you to spend the rest of your afterlives. Thank you, trees, for your heroic sacrifice. You're American now.

In your debt,   With deepest respect,

The authors   *Publisher*

ABOUT THE AUTHORS

Chris Ying was b⬛⬛⬛⬛⬛⬛⬛ he was raised by a mother and a father. He was a baby at one p⬛⬛⬛⬛⬛⬛ finally an adult. He attended the University of California⬛⬛⬛⬛⬛ favorite beginning with pet dander.

Brian McMullen lives in the⬛⬛⬛⬛⬛⬛ on the edge of San Francisco. He was born in Toledo, Ohio in⬛⬛⬛⬛⬛ of brownie on the wall of the school bathroom. A secret: Brian loves to e⬛⬛⬛⬛⬛ve it, period.